Easy Entertaining

Publications International, Ltd.

Favorite Brand Name Recipes at www.fbnr.com

Pictured on the front cover: Eggplant Parmigiana *(page 60).*
Pictured on the back cover: Apple Crunch Pie *(page 112).*

Microwave Cooking: Microwave ovens vary in wattage. Use the cooking times as guidelines and check for doneness before adding more time.

Preparation/Cooking Times: Preparation times are based on the approximate amount of time required to assemble the recipe before cooking, baking, chilling or serving. These times include preparation steps such as measuring, chopping and mixing. The fact that some preparations and cooking can be done simultaneously is taken into account. Preparation of optional ingredients and serving suggestions is not included.

Table of Contents

Sunrise Brunch 4

Simple Starters 28

Pleasing Main Dishes 48

On the Side 78

Ravishing Desserts 106

Bottoms Up Beverages 140

Acknowledgments 154

Index 155

Donut Spice Cakes

1 package (9 ounces) yellow cake mix
½ cup cold water
2 eggs
½ teaspoon ground cinnamon
¼ teaspoon ground nutmeg
2 teaspoons powdered sugar

1. Preheat oven to 350°F. Grease and flour 10 (½-cup) mini bundt pans.

2. Combine cake mix, water, eggs, cinnamon and nutmeg in medium bowl. Beat with electric mixer at high speed 4 minutes or until well blended.

3. Spoon about ¼ cup batter into each prepared bundt pan cup. Bake 13 minutes or until toothpicks inserted near centers come out clean and cakes spring back when lightly touched.

4. Cool in pans on wire racks 5 minutes. Remove cakes from pans. Serve warm or at room temperature. Sprinkle with powdered sugar just before serving. *Makes 10 servings*

Prep Time: 10 minutes
Bake Time: 13 minutes

Donut Spice Cakes

Mini Pumpkin Cranberry Breads

3 cups all-purpose flour
1 tablespoon plus 2 teaspoons pumpkin pie spice
2 teaspoons baking soda
1½ teaspoons salt
3 cups granulated sugar
1 can (15 ounces) LIBBY'S® 100% Pure Pumpkin
4 large eggs
1 cup vegetable oil
½ cup orange juice or water
1 cup sweetened dried, fresh or frozen cranberries

PREHEAT oven to 350°F. Grease and flour five or six 5×3-inch mini disposable or meat loaf pans.

COMBINE flour, pumpkin pie spice, baking soda and salt in large bowl. Combine sugar, pumpkin, eggs, vegetable oil and orange juice in large mixer bowl; beat until just blended. Add pumpkin mixture to flour mixture; stir just until moistened. Fold in cranberries. Spoon batter into prepared loaf pans.

BAKE for 50 to 55 minutes or until wooden pick inserted in center comes out clean. Cool in pans on wire racks for 10 minutes; remove to wire racks to cool completely. *Makes 5 or 6 mini loaves*

Helpful Hint

If you don't have pumpkin pie spice, combine 1½ teaspoons ground cinnamon, 1¼ teaspoons ground ginger and ½ teaspoon each ground allspice and nutmeg for the 1 tablespoon plus 2 teaspoons.

Mini Pumpkin Cranberry Bread

Ham and Swiss Quiche

1 *unbaked* 9-inch (4-cup volume) deep-dish pie shell
1 cup (4 ounces) shredded Swiss cheese, *divided*
1 cup finely chopped cooked ham
2 green onions, sliced
1 can (12 fluid ounces) NESTLÉ® CARNATION® Evaporated Milk
3 large eggs
¼ cup all-purpose flour
¼ teaspoon salt
⅛ teaspoon ground black pepper

PREHEAT oven to 350°F.

SPRINKLE *½ cup* cheese, ham and green onions into pie crust. Whisk together evaporated milk, eggs, flour, salt and pepper in large bowl. Pour mixture into pie shell; sprinkle with *remaining* cheese.

BAKE for 45 to 50 minutes or until knife inserted near center comes out clean. Cool on wire rack for 10 minutes before serving.

Makes 8 servings

For Mini-Quiche Appetizers: Use 1½ packages (3 crusts) refrigerated pie crusts. Grease miniature muffin pans. Unfold crust on lightly floured surface. Cut fourteen 2½-inch circles from each crust. Press 1 circle of dough into bottom and up side of each cup. Repeat with *remaining* crusts. Combine cheese, ham, green onions, ⅔ *cup (5-fluid-ounce can)* evaporated milk, 2 eggs (lightly beaten), *2 tablespoons* flour, salt and pepper in large bowl; mix well. Spoon mixture into crusts, filling ¾ full. Bake in preheated 350°F. oven for 20 to 25 minutes or until crusts are golden brown. Cool slightly; lift quiche from cup with tip of knife. Serve warm or cool and freeze for later entertaining. Makes 3½ dozen.

Ham and Swiss Quiche

Spiced Pancakes with Apple Topping

¼ cup I CAN'T BELIEVE IT'S NOT BUTTER!® Spread
¼ cup sugar
¾ cup apple juice
¼ cup pure maple syrup or pancake syrup
3 large apples, cored, peeled and cut into ½-inch slices
1 cup original pancake and waffle mix OR 1 container (16 ounces) frozen pancake batter, thawed
½ teaspoon ground cinnamon
½ teaspoon vanilla extract
¼ teaspoon ground ginger (optional)
2 teaspoons cornstarch

In 12-inch nonstick skillet, melt I Can't Believe It's Not Butter!® Spread and cook sugar, ½ cup apple juice, syrup and apples over medium heat, stirring occasionally, 15 minutes or until apples are tender.

Meanwhile, prepare pancake mix according to package directions, blending in cinnamon, vanilla and ginger. In another 12-inch nonstick skillet or on griddle, cook pancakes until done, turning once.

In small bowl, with wire whisk, blend remaining ¼ cup apple juice and cornstarch. Add to apples and bring to a boil over high heat. Boil, stirring occasionally, 1 minute or until thickened. Serve with pancakes topped with I Can't Believe It's Not Butter!® Spread and pancake syrup.

Makes 4 servings

Prep Time: 10 minutes
Cook Time: 20 minutes

Spiced Pancakes with Apple Topping

Donna's Heavenly Orange Chip Scones

4 cups all-purpose flour
1 cup granulated sugar
4 teaspoons baking powder
½ teaspoon baking soda
½ teaspoon salt
1 cup (6 ounces) NESTLÉ® TOLL HOUSE® Semi-Sweet Chocolate
    Mini Morsels
1 cup golden raisins
1 tablespoon grated orange peel
1 cup (2 sticks) unsalted butter, cut into pieces and softened
1 cup buttermilk
3 large eggs, *divided*
1 teaspoon orange extract
1 tablespoon milk
    Icing (recipe follows)

PREHEAT oven to 350°F. Lightly grease baking sheets.

COMBINE flour, granulated sugar, baking powder, baking soda and salt in large bowl. Add morsels, raisins and orange peel; mix well. Cut in butter with pastry blender or two knives until mixture resembles coarse crumbs. Combine buttermilk, *2 eggs* and orange extract in small bowl. Pour buttermilk mixture into flour mixture; mix just until a sticky dough is formed. Do not overmix. Drop by ¼ cupfuls onto prepared baking sheets. Combine *remaining* egg and milk in small bowl. Brush egg mixture over top of dough.

BAKE for 18 to 22 minutes or until wooden pick inserted in center comes out clean. For best results, bake one baking sheet at a time. Cool on wire racks for 10 minutes. Drizzle scones with icing. Serve warm.

Makes 2 dozen scones

Icing: **COMBINE** 2 cups powdered sugar, ¼ cup orange juice, 1 tablespoon grated orange peel and 1 teaspoon orange extract in medium bowl. Mix until smooth.

Donna's Heavenly Orange Chip Scones

Chile Rellenos Monte Cristos

1 can (4 ounces) whole roasted green chiles
8 large slices sourdough bread
4 slices SARGENTO® Deli Style Sliced Monterey Jack Cheese
4 slices SARGENTO® Deli Style Sliced Colby Cheese
2 eggs
¼ cup milk
1 teaspoon ground cumin
¼ cup butter or margarine
   Powdered sugar, optional
   Thick and chunky salsa, optional

1. Cut open chiles and remove any remaining seeds. Equally divide the chiles over 4 slices of bread. Top each with Monterey Jack and Colby cheeses. Place remaining bread slices on top.

2. In shallow bowl, beat eggs, milk and cumin until blended. Dip each sandwich in the egg mixture, turning carefully to coat until all liquid is absorbed by all sandwiches equally.

3. Melt butter in large skillet over medium heat. Place sandwiches in skillet. Grill (in batches if necessary) 3 to 4 minutes per side, or until browned and cheese has melted. Serve immediately. Serve with powdered sugar sprinkled on top and a spoonful of salsa, if desired.

Makes 4 servings

Prep Time: 5 minutes
Cook Time: 16 minutes

Chile Rellenos Monte Cristo

Cinnamon Spiced Muffins

1½ cups all-purpose flour
¾ cup sugar, divided
2 teaspoons baking powder
½ teaspoon salt
½ teaspoon ground nutmeg
½ teaspoon ground coriander
½ teaspoon ground allspice
½ cup milk
⅓ cup butter, melted
1 egg
1 teaspoon ground cinnamon
¼ cup butter, melted

1. Preheat oven to 400°F. Grease 36 (1¾-inch) mini muffin cups.

2. Combine flour, ½ cup sugar, baking powder, salt, nutmeg, coriander and allspice in large bowl. Combine milk, butter and egg in small bowl; stir into flour mixture just until moistened. Spoon evenly into prepared muffin cups.

3. Bake 10 to 13 minutes or until edges are lightly browned and toothpick inserted in center comes out clean. Remove from pan.

4. Meanwhile, combine remaining ¼ cup sugar and cinnamon in shallow dish. Dip warm muffin tops in remaining ¼ cup melted butter, then in sugar-cinnamon mixture. Serve warm.   *Makes 36 mini muffins*

Helpful Hint

*Don't stir muffin batter too much—
overmixing will make the muffins tough.
There should still be lumps in the batter;
these will disappear during baking.*

Cinnamon Spiced Muffins

Stuffed French Toast with Fresh Berry Topping

2 cups mixed fresh berries (strawberries, raspberries, blueberries and/or blackberries)
2 tablespoons granulated sugar
⅔ cup lowfat ricotta cheese
¼ cup strawberry preserves
3 large eggs
⅔ cup (5-ounce can) NESTLÉ® CARNATION® Evaporated Fat Free Milk
2 tablespoons packed brown sugar
2 teaspoons vanilla extract
12 slices (about ¾ inch thick) French bread
1 tablespoon vegetable oil, butter or margarine
Powdered sugar (optional)
Maple syrup, heated (optional)

COMBINE berries and granulated sugar in small bowl. Combine ricotta cheese and strawberry preserves in another small bowl; mix well. Combine eggs, evaporated milk, brown sugar and vanilla extract in pie plate or shallow bowl; mix well.

SPREAD ricotta-preserve mixture evenly over *6 slices* of bread. Top with *remaining* slices of bread to form sandwiches.

HEAT vegetable oil or butter in large, nonstick skillet or griddle over medium heat. Dip sandwiches in egg mixture, coating both sides. Cook on each side for about 2 minutes or until golden brown.

SPRINKLE with powdered sugar; top with berries. Serve with maple syrup, if desired   *Makes 6 servings*

Stuffed French Toast with Fresh Berry Topping

Lots o' Chocolate Bread

⅔ cup packed light brown sugar
½ cup (1 stick) butter, softened
2 cups miniature semisweet chocolate chips, divided
2 eggs
2½ cups all-purpose flour
1½ cups applesauce
1½ teaspoons vanilla
1 teaspoon baking soda
1 teaspoon baking powder
½ teaspoon salt
1 tablespoon shortening (do not use butter, margarine, spread or oil)

1. Preheat oven to 350°F. Grease 5 (5½×3-inch) mini loaf pans. Beat brown sugar and butter in large bowl with electric mixer until creamy. Melt 1 cup miniature chocolate chips; cool slightly and add to sugar mixture with eggs. Add flour, applesauce, vanilla, baking soda, baking powder and salt; beat until well mixed. Stir in ½ cup chocolate chips. Spoon batter into prepared pans; bake 35 to 40 minutes or until centers crack and are dry to the touch. Cool 10 minutes before removing from pans.

2. Place remaining ½ cup chocolate chips and shortening in small microwavable bowl. Microwave at HIGH 1 minute; stir. If necessary, microwave at HIGH an additional 15 seconds at a time, stirring after each heating. Drizzle warm loaves with glaze. Cool completely.

Makes 5 mini loaves

Lots o' Chocolate Bread

Brunch Sausage Casserole

4 cups cubed day-old bread
2 cups (8 ounces) shredded sharp cheddar cheese
2 cans (12 fluid ounces *each*) NESTLÉ® CARNATION® Evaporated
    Milk
10 large eggs, lightly beaten
1 teaspoon dry mustard
¼ teaspoon onion powder
    Ground black pepper to taste
1 package (16 ounces) fresh breakfast sausage, cooked, drained and
    crumbled

GREASE 13×9-inch baking dish. Place bread in prepared baking dish. Sprinkle with cheese. Combine evaporated milk, eggs, dry mustard, onion powder and pepper in medium bowl. Pour evenly over bread and cheese. Sprinkle with sausage. Cover; refrigerate overnight.

PREHEAT oven to 325°F.

BAKE for 55 to 60 minutes or until cheese is golden brown. Cover with foil if top browns too quickly.   *Makes 10 to 12 servings*

Hash Brown Bake

1 packet (1 ounce) HIDDEN VALLEY® The Original Ranch® Salad
    Dressing & Seasoning Mix
1¼ cups milk
3 ounces cream cheese
6 cups hash browns (frozen shredded potatoes)
1 tablespoon bacon bits
½ cup shredded sharp Cheddar cheese

In blender, combine salad dressing & seasoning mix, milk and cream cheese. Pour over potatoes and bacon bits in 9-inch baking dish. Top with cheese. Bake at 350°F for 35 minutes.   *Makes 4 servings*

Huevos Rancheros in Tortilla Cups

Olive oil cooking spray
6 taco-size corn tortillas, about 6-inch diameter
1 can (14½ ounces) diced tomatoes
1 can (8 ounces) no salt added tomato sauce
1 can (4 ounces) diced mild green chilies
⅓ cup *Frank's® RedHot®* Original Cayenne Pepper Sauce
½ to 1 teaspoon ground cumin
6 large eggs
1 cup shredded Mexican 4-cheese blend
Garnish (optional): cilantro, black beans

1. Preheat oven to 425°F. Place tortillas in damp paper towels. Soften in microwave for 30 seconds. Coat both sides of tortillas with cooking spray. Place tortillas into 10-ounce custard cups, pressing in sides. Place a ball of foil in center to hold in sides of tortillas. Bake 15 minutes until golden. Cool tortilla cups on rack and remove foil.

2. In 12-inch ovenproof skillet combine tomatoes, tomato sauce, chilies, **Frank's RedHot** Sauce and cumin. Bring to a boil. Simmer for 4 minutes until flavors are blended. Remove from heat. With large spoon, make an indentation in sauce; pour 1 egg into indentation. Repeat with remaining eggs.

3. Bake 7 minutes more or until eggs are almost set. Sprinkle cheese over eggs and bake 1 minute or until melted. To serve, spoon sauce and eggs into tortilla cups. Garnish with cilantro and black beans, if desired.

Makes 6 servings

Prep Time: 10 minutes
Cook Time: 25 minutes

Individual Spinach & Bacon Quiches

3 slices bacon
½ small onion, diced
1 package (9 ounces) frozen chopped spinach, thawed, drained and
   squeezed dry
½ teaspoon black pepper
⅛ teaspoon ground nutmeg
   Pinch salt
1 container (15 ounces) whole milk ricotta cheese
2 cups (8 ounces) shredded mozzarella cheese
1 cup (4 ounces) grated Parmesan cheese
3 eggs, lightly beaten

1. Preheat oven to 350°F. Spray 10 muffin pan cups with nonstick cooking spray.

2. Cook bacon in large skillet over medium-high heat until crisp. Drain; let cool and crumble.

3. In same skillet, cook and stir onion in remaining bacon fat 5 minutes or until tender. Add spinach, pepper, nutmeg and salt. Cook and stir over medium heat about 3 minutes or until liquid evaporates. Remove from heat. Stir in bacon; let cool.

4. Combine ricotta, mozzarella and Parmesan cheeses in large bowl. Add eggs; stir until well blended. Add cooled spinach mixture; mix well.

5. Divide mixture evenly among prepared muffin cups. Bake 40 minutes or until set. Let stand 10 minutes. Run thin knife around edges to release. Serve hot or refrigerate and serve cold.   *Makes 10 servings*

Individual Spinach & Bacon Quiches

Hawaiian Fruit and Nut Quick Bread

2 cups all-purpose flour
1 tablespoon orange-flavored instant drink powder
2 teaspoons baking soda
1 teaspoon cinnamon
¾ cup granulated sugar
¾ cup light brown sugar
¾ cup chopped macadamia nuts
½ cup shredded coconut
¾ cup canola oil
2 eggs
2 teaspoons rum extract
2 cups chopped fresh mango

1. Preheat oven to 350°F. Lightly grease 9×3-inch loaf pan. Set aside.

2. Sift flour, drink powder, baking soda and cinnamon into medium bowl. Stir in sugars, macadamia nuts and coconut. Combine oil, eggs and rum extract in separate medium bowl. Add to dry mixture; stir to mix well. Stir in mango.

3. Spoon batter into prepared pan. Bake 60 to 70 minutes or until bread is light golden brown in color and pulls away from sides of pan. Cool in pan 10 minutes. Remove to wire rack; cool completely.   *Makes 1 loaf*

Entertaining Idea

Add a special touch to your breakfast buffet by serving flavored creamers, brownulated sugar, ground cinnamon and ground nutmeg for your guests to add to their coffee.

Hawaiian Fruit and Nut Quick Bread

California Veggie Rolls

1 package (8 ounces) cream cheese, softened
½ teaspoon LAWRY'S® Garlic Powder With Parsley
½ teaspoon LAWRY'S® Lemon Pepper
6 large (burrito size) *or* 12 soft taco size flour tortillas, warmed to soften
1 large bunch fresh spinach leaves, cleaned and stems removed
1½ cups (6 ounces) shredded cheddar cheese
1½ cups shredded carrot
Fresh salsa

In small bowl, mix together cream cheese, Garlic Powder With Parsley and Lemon Pepper. On each flour tortilla, spread a layer of cream cheese mixture. Layer on spinach leaves, cheddar cheese and carrot. Roll up tortilla and secure with toothpick. Slice each roll into 1½-inch pieces. Serve with fresh salsa.   *Makes 3 dozen rolls*

Variation: Adding sliced deli meat or adding Dijon mustard to the cream cheese will give variety to these rolls.

Hint: To keep tortillas soft until slicing, wrap tightly in plastic wrap or cover with damp towel.

Prep. Time: 20 minutes

California Veggie Rolls

Buffalo Chicken Wing Sampler

2½ **pounds chicken wing pieces**
½ **cup** *Frank's® RedHot®* **Original Cayenne Pepper Sauce**
⅓ **cup melted butter**

1. Deep-fry* wings in hot oil (400°F) for 12 minutes until fully cooked and crispy; drain.

2. Combine *Frank's RedHot* Sauce and butter. Dip wings in sauce to coat.

3. Serve wings with celery and blue cheese dressing if desired.

Makes 8 appetizer servings

For equally crispy wings, bake 1 hour at 425°F, or grill 30 minutes over medium heat.

RedHot® Sampler Variations: Add one of the following to *RedHot* butter mixture; heat through. Tex-Mex: 1 tablespoon chili powder; ¼ teaspoon garlic powder. Asian: 2 tablespoons honey, 2 tablespoons teriyaki sauce, 2 teaspoons ground ginger. Sprinkle wings with 1 tablespoon sesame seeds. Zesty Honey-Dijon: Substitute the following blend instead of the *RedHot* butter mixture: ¼ cup each *Frank's® RedHot®* Sauce, *French's®* Honey Dijon Mustard and honey.

Prep Time: 5 minutes
Cook Time: 12 minutes

Entertaining Idea

To get the party started play a variety of
background music everyone will enjoy.
Choose selections from R&B to classical
to jazz.

Buffalo Chicken Wing Sampler

Tomato and Caper Crostini

1 French roll, cut into 8 slices (about 1½ ounces)
2 plum tomatoes, finely chopped (about 4 ounces)
1½ tablespoons capers
1½ teaspoons dried basil leaves
1 teaspoon extra-virgin olive oil
1 ounce crumbled feta (any variety, preferably sun-dried tomatoes
and basil)

1. Preheat oven 350°F.

2. Place bread slices on baking sheet in a single layer. Bake 15 minutes or until just golden brown. Remove from oven; let cool completely.

3. Meanwhile, in a small bowl, combine tomatoes, capers, basil and oil.

4. To serve, spoon tomato mixture on each bread slice and sprinkle cheese on top.

Makes 4 servings

Helpful Hint

In season, tomatoes should be plump and heavy with a vibrant color and a pleasant aroma. They should be firm but not hard. A soft tomato will either be watery or overripe. Avoid those that are cracked or have soft spots.

Tomato and Caper Crostini

Crab Cakes with Horseradish Mustard Sauce

Horseradish Mustard Sauce
- 1/2 cup mayonnaise
- 2 tablespoons *French's®* Honey Dijon Mustard
- 1 tablespoon prepared horseradish

Crab Cakes
- 1 1/3 cups *French's®* French Fried Onions, divided
- 3 cans (6 ounces each) jumbo lump crabmeat, drained
- 1/4 cup unseasoned dry bread crumbs
- 1/4 cup mayonnaise
- 1 egg, slightly beaten
- 2 tablespoons chopped pimientos
- 2 tablespoons chopped parsley
- 1 tablespoon *French's®* Honey Dijon Mustard
- 1 tablespoon prepared horseradish
- 1 teaspoon minced garlic

1. Combine ingredients for Horseradish Mustard Sauce in small bowl. Chill until ready to serve.

2. Lightly crush 2/3 cup French Fried Onions. Place in large bowl. Add remaining ingredients for crab cakes; mix until well combined. Shape mixture into cakes using about 1/4 cup mixture for each; flatten slightly.

3. Heat 2 tablespoons oil in 12-inch nonstick skillet over medium high heat. Cook crab cakes in batches, about 2 to 3 minutes per side or until golden. Drain. Transfer crab cakes to serving platter. Serve each crab cake topped with Horseradish Mustard Sauce and remaining onions.

Makes about 12 crab cakes

Prep Time: 15 minutes
Cook Time: 12 minutes

Santa Fe Shrimp Martini Cocktails (page 36) and
Crab Cakes with Horseradish Mustard Sauce

Santa Fe Shrimp Martini Cocktails

1 jar (16 ounces) mild salsa
1 ripe small avocado, peeled and chopped
1 tablespoon *Frank's® RedHot®* Original Cayenne Pepper Sauce
1 tablespoon lime juice
1 tablespoon chopped fresh cilantro leaves
1 pound large shrimp, cooked, peeled and deveined
1 cup *French's®* French Fried Onions
1 lime, cut into 6 wedges

1. Combine salsa, avocado, **Frank's RedHot** Sauce, lime juice and cilantro in large bowl. Alternately layer shrimp and salsa mixture in 6 margarita or martini glasses.

2. Microwave French Fried Onions on HIGH for 1 minute until golden. Sprinkle over shrimp. Garnish with lime wedges.   *Makes 6 servings*

Quick Tip: Purchase cooked, cleaned shrimp from the seafood section of your local supermarket.

Prep Time: 10 minutes
Cook Time: 1 minute

Marinated Chicken Satay with Peanut Butter Dipping Sauce

CHICKEN AND MARINADE
- 2 tablespoons JIF® Creamy Peanut Butter
- ½ cup Italian salad dressing
- 1 pound skinless, boneless chicken breasts, cut into ½×4-inch strips
- 10 to 12 wooden skewers (soak in warm water for 30 minutes prior to use)

DIPPING SAUCE
- ½ cup JIF® Creamy Peanut Butter
- 6 tablespoons water
- ½ cup parsley or cilantro leaves, chopped
- 3 tablespoons fresh lime juice
- 2 tablespoons reduced-sodium soy sauce
- 1 tablespoon honey
- 1 teaspoon sesame oil
- Pinch cayenne powder

In a medium-sized bowl, whisk together the JIF® peanut butter and salad dressing until smooth. Place chicken strips in mixture. Marinate in covered bowl 3 hours or overnight in refrigerator.

Heat broiler to high. Remove chicken from refrigerator. Thread 2 chicken strips onto a skewer. Arrange skewers on a metal grill rack positioned over a foil-lined baking pan. Broil skewers 6 minutes; turn skewers over. Broil another 4 to 6 minutes or until juices run clear and chicken is thoroughly cooked. Serve chicken skewers with dipping sauce, if desired.

To prepare the dipping sauce, place all ingredients in a blender; blend on medium-high until smooth. *Make 3 to 4 servings*

Note: To grill, place skewered chicken on hot grill for 8 minutes, or until juices run clear.

Substitution: Substitute 2 pounds of beef or shrimp for the chicken in the above recipe, or better yet, serve a mixture of all three at your next party!

Apricot BBQ Glazed Shrimp and Bacon

1 (8-ounce) can sliced water chestnuts, drained
36 medium raw shrimp, peeled and deveined (about 1¼ pounds)
9 bacon slices, each cut into 4 pieces
⅓ cup barbecue sauce
⅓ cup apricot fruit spread
1 tablespoon grated ginger
1 tablespoon cider vinegar
⅛ teaspoon dried red pepper flakes

1. Preheat broiler. Place 1 water chestnut slice on top of each shrimp. Wrap 1 piece of bacon around shrimp and secure with wooden toothpick. Repeat with remaining water chestnuts, shrimp and bacon.

2. Line broiler pan with foil; insert broiler rack. Coat broiler rack with nonstick cooking spray. Arrange shrimp on rack.

3. Combine remaining ingredients in small mixing bowl and set aside. Brush sauce evenly over each shrimp and broil 2 minutes; turn. Baste and broil 2 minutes more; turn again. Baste and broil 1 minute more, or until edges of bacon are beginning to brown. *Makes 36 appetizers*

Helpful Hint

To devein shrimp, make a small cut along the back and lift out the dark vein with the tip of a knife. You may find the task easier if it is done under cold running water.

Apricot BBQ Glazed Shrimp and Bacon

Spinach-Artichoke Party Cups

Nonstick cooking spray
36 (3-inch) wonton wrappers
1 can (8½ ounces) artichoke hearts, drained and chopped
½ package (10 ounces) frozen chopped spinach, thawed and squeezed dry
1 cup shredded Monterey Jack cheese
½ cup grated Parmesan cheese
½ cup mayonnaise
1 clove garlic, minced

1. Preheat oven to 300°F. Spray miniature muffin pan lightly with cooking spray. Press 1 wonton wrapper into each cup; spray lightly with cooking spray. Bake about 9 minutes or until light golden brown. Remove shells from muffin pan; set aside to cool. Repeat with remaining wonton wrappers.*

2. Meanwhile, combine artichoke hearts, spinach, cheeses, mayonnaise and garlic in medium bowl; mix well.

3. Fill each wonton cup with about 1½ teaspoons spinach-artichoke mixture. Place filled cups on baking sheet. Bake about 7 minutes or until heated through. Serve immediately.   *Makes 36 appetizers*

Wonton cups may be prepared up to one week in advance. Cool completely and store in an airtight container.

Tip: If you have leftover spinach-artichoke mixture after filling the wonton cups, place the mixture in a shallow ovenproof dish and bake it at 350°F until hot and bubbly. Serve it with bread or crackers.

Spinach-Artichoke Party Cups

Angel Wings

1 can (10¾ ounces) condensed tomato soup, undiluted
¾ cup water
¼ cup packed light brown sugar
2½ tablespoons balsamic vinegar
2 tablespoons chopped shallots
10 chicken wings

Slow Cooker Directions

1. Combine soup, water, brown sugar, vinegar and shallots in slow cooker; mix well.

2. Add chicken wings; stir to coat with sauce. Cover; cook on LOW 5 to 6 hours or until cooked through and glazed with sauce.   *Makes 2 servings*

Alouette Garlic and Herb Croustade

2 (2-ounce) packages mini phyllo shells
1 tablespoon olive oil
1 teaspoon garlic, chopped
½ cup onion, minced
⅔ cup red bell pepper, roasted, chopped
1 cup baby bella or other mushroom, chopped
½ cup bacon, blanched and chopped
1 (6.5-ounce) or 2 (4-ounce) packages ALOUETTE® Garlic et Herbes
2 tablespoons chopped fresh parsley (or 1 tablespoon dried)

In a non-stick pan over medium heat, heat oil and sauté garlic, onion, pepper, mushroom and bacon for 3 to 5 minutes. Reduce heat to low and add Alouette. Blend and simmer for a minute. Remove from heat and stir in parsley. Spoon a heaping teaspoon in each phyllo cup and serve warm.

Makes 30 appetizers

Tip: For a creative touch, use any variety of seasonally fresh vegetables such as chopped fennel, summer or winter squash, etc

Angel Wings

Mediterranean Roast Tomatoes

2 small to medium beefsteak tomatoes, halved crosswise
4 fresh basil leaves
2 tablespoons finely chopped pitted kalamata olives
2 tablespoons shredded mozzarella cheese
2 tablespoons grated Parmesan cheese

1. Preheat toaster oven to broil. Place tomato halves on rack on toaster oven tray or on toaster-sized broiler pan. Top each tomato half with 1 fresh basil leaf, ½ tablespoon olives, ½ tablespoon mozzarella cheese and ½ tablespoon Parmesan cheese.

2. Broil in toaster oven for 2 minutes or until cheese melts and begins to brown. Remove from oven and cool slightly before serving.

Makes 4 servings

Helpful Hint

To make these tasty tomatoes for a big crowd, simply double or triple the recipe. Broil in conventional oven instead of toaster oven.

Mediterranean Roast Tomatoes

Walnut-Crusted Salmon Bites with Apricot Ginger Dipping Sauce

Non-stick cooking spray
¼ cup apricot jam
2 tablespoons white balsamic vinegar or white wine vinegar
¾ cup chopped California walnuts
¾ cup pankow bread crumbs (available in Asian markets) or regular, seasoned breadcrumbs
2 tablespoons chopped cilantro
1 pound skinless salmon fillet, cut into 1-inch cubes
Apricot Ginger Dipping Sauce (recipe follows)

Preheat oven to 400°F. Coat a baking sheet with non-stick cooking spray. Whisk together jam and vinegar; set aside. In a blender, combine walnuts, bread crumbs and cilantro. Process a few turns until blended but still a coarse texture. Brush salmon pieces with the jam mixture. Coat evenly with the walnut mixture. Place on prepared sheet and bake for 12 minutes. Serve with Apricot Ginger Dipping Sauce.   *Makes 8 servings*

Apricot Ginger Dipping Sauce

½ cup apricot jam
2 tablespoons water
2 tablespoons finely chopped California walnuts
4 teaspoons low sodium soy sauce
1 tablespoon thinly sliced green onion, white and pale green part
1 teaspoon minced ginger
1 teaspoon white balsamic vinegar

In a small bowl, whisk together all ingredients. Serve with crispy salmon bites.   *Makes about ¾ cup*

Favorite recipe from **Walnut Marketing Board**

Mediterranean Sausage and Spinach Tartlets

1 (16-ounce) package PERDUE® Fresh Seasoned Lean Turkey
    Sausage, Sweet Italian
½ cup frozen chopped spinach, thawed and squeezed dry
1 cup crumbled feta cheese
2 green onions, minced
1½ teaspoons fresh oregano, chopped
    Salt and pepper, to taste
2 (2.1 ounce) packages mini fillo dough shells
15 pitted kalamata olives, halved

Preheat oven to 375°F.

Remove sausage from casing and place in a large, non-stick skillet over high heat. Sauté until cooked through, breaking up sausage with a wooden spoon as it cooks. Stir in spinach until hot. Turn off heat, stir in feta, green onion, oregano, and salt and pepper to taste.

Set fillo cups on a sheetpan and bake them until crisp and hot, about 4 minutes. Fill each cup with sausage mixture and top with an olive half. Serve immediately. *Makes 30 appetizers*

Prep Time: 30 minutes
Cook Time: 10 minutes

Grilled Tequila Lime Salmon

1 cup LAWRY'S® Tequila Lime Marinade With Lime Juice, divided
1 pound fresh salmon fillet or steaks
1 lime, cut into wedges (optional garnish)
   Fresh cilantro sprigs (optional garnish)

In large resealable plastic bag, combine ¾ cup Tequila Lime Marinade and salmon, seal bag. Marinate in refrigerator for 30 minutes, turning occasionally. Remove salmon from bag, discarding used Marinade. Grill salmon until opaque and fish begins to flake easily, for 8 to 10 minutes, brushing often with remaining Marinade. Serve with lime wedges and fresh cilantro for garnish, if desired.   *Makes 4 servings*

Meal Idea: Serve with black beans, rice and warm tortillas.

Prep. Time: 5 minutes
Marinate Time: 30 minutes
Cook Time: 8 to 10 minutes

Grilled Tequila Lime Salmon

Parmesan Turkey Breast

½ teaspoon salt
¼ teaspoon black pepper
1 pound turkey breast, chicken breasts or veal cutlets, cut ⅛ to
    ¼ inch thick
2 tablespoons butter, melted
2 cloves garlic, minced
½ cup grated Parmesan cheese
1 cup marinara sauce, warmed
2 tablespoons chopped fresh basil

Preheat broiler. Sprinkle salt and pepper over turkey. Place turkey in
1 layer in 15×10×1-inch pan. Combine butter and garlic in small bowl;
brush over turkey. Broil turkey 4 to 5 inches from heat source 2 minutes;
turn. Sprinkle with cheese. Broil 2 to 3 minutes or until turkey is no longer
pink in center. Transfer to serving plates. Spoon marinara sauce over
turkey; sprinkle with basil.   *Makes 4 servings*

Variation: Preheat oven to 350°F. Sprinkle salt and pepper over turkey.
Brown turkey on both sides in 1 to 2 tablespoons hot oil in a medium
skillet. Place browned turkey in small casserole or 9×9-inch baking dish.
Top with marinara sauce; cover pan with foil. Bake turkey 30 minutes or
until no longer pink in center. Remove from oven and remove foil; sprinkle
with Parmesan cheese and basil.

Entertaining Idea

*For place settings with a personal touch, set
small photo frames at each place with a
favorite picture of each guest. If you don't
have photos of everybody, you can opt to
write guests' names in the frames instead.*

Parmesan Turkey Breast

Bodacious Grilled Ribs

4 pounds pork loin back ribs
2 tablespoons paprika
2 teaspoons dried basil leaves
½ teaspoon onion powder
¼ teaspoon garlic powder
¼ teaspoon ground red pepper
¼ teaspoon black pepper
2 sheets (24×18 inches) heavy-duty foil, lightly sprayed with
    nonstick cooking spray
8 ice cubes
1 cup barbecue sauce
½ cup apricot all-fruit spread

1. Prepare grill for direct cooking. Cut ribs into 4- to 6-rib pieces.

2. Combine paprika, basil, onion powder, garlic powder, red pepper and black pepper in small bowl. Rub on both sides of rib pieces. Place half of ribs in single layer in center of each foil sheet. Place 4 ice cubes on top of each.

3. Double fold sides and ends of foil to seal packets, leaving head space for heat circulation. Place on baking sheet. Stir together barbecue sauce and jam; set aside.

4. Slide packets off baking sheet onto grill grid. Grill, covered, over medium coals 45 to 60 minutes or until tender. Carefully open one end of each packet to allow steam to escape.

5. Open packets and transfer ribs to grill rack. Brush with barbecue sauce mixture. Continue grilling 5 to 10 minutes, brushing with sauce and turning often.

Makes 4 servings

Bodacious Grilled Ribs

Saucy Tomato Chicken

6 ounces uncooked yolk-free egg noodles
1 can (14½ ounces) stewed tomatoes with onions, celery and green
    bell pepper
2 cloves garlic, minced
1 teaspoon dried oregano leaves
   Nonstick cooking spray
4 boneless skinless chicken breasts (4 ounces each), rinsed and
    patted dry
2 teaspoons olive oil

1. Cook noodles according to package directions, omitting salt and oil; drain.

2. Meanwhile, heat large nonstick skillet over high heat; add tomatoes, garlic and oregano. Bring to a boil over high heat; boil 5 minutes, stirring constantly, or until liquid is reduced and tomato mixture becomes slightly darker in color. (Mixture will be thick.) Transfer to small bowl and keep warm. Wipe out skillet.

3. Spray same skillet with cooking spray. Add chicken and cook 6 minutes. Turn; reduce heat to medium-low. Spoon tomato mixture into skillet around chicken. Cover and cook 4 minutes or until chicken is no longer pink in center and juices run clear.

4. Remove skillet from heat. Place noodles on serving platter and top with chicken pieces. Add olive oil to tomato mixture in skillet and stir well to blend. Spoon tomato mixture over chicken. *Makes 4 servings*

Saucy Tomato Chicken

Seafood Parmesan

2 tablespoons margarine or butter
1 pound uncooked large shrimp, peeled and deveined
2 cloves garlic, minced
1 teaspoon paprika
⅛ to ¼ teaspoon cayenne pepper
1 (4.6-ounce) package PASTA RONI® Garlic & Olive Oil with
    Vermicelli
¾ cup frozen or canned peas, drained
¼ cup grated Parmesan cheese

1. In large saucepan over medium heat, melt margarine. Add shrimp, garlic, paprika and cayenne pepper; sauté 2 minutes. Remove from saucepan; set aside.

2. In same saucepan, bring 1¾ cups water to a boil. Slowly stir in pasta and Special Seasonings; reduce heat to medium. Gently boil uncovered, 6 minutes, stirring occasionally.

3. Stir in shrimp mixture and peas; boil 3 to 4 minutes or until pasta is tender, stirring frequently. Let stand 5 minutes before serving. Serve with cheese.   *Makes 4 servings*

Prep Time: 5 minutes
Cook Time: 20 minutes

Helpful Hint

To devein shrimp, make a small cut along the back of the shrimp; lift out the dark vein with the tip of a knife under cold running water.

Seafood Parmesan

Asian Grilled Steaks with Spicy Herb Sauce

⅔ cup CRISCO® Oil
3 tablespoons sugar
3 tablespoons cooking sherry
1 tablespoon plus 1½ teaspoons minced garlic
1 tablespoon dark sesame oil
1 teaspoon red pepper flakes
½ teaspoon salt
6 (1-inch-thick) strip steaks
   Salt and black pepper, to taste

Spicy Herb Sauce
1 cup chopped cilantro, including stems
⅓ cup CRISCO® Oil
3 tablespoons soy sauce
1 tablespoon fresh lime juice
1½ teaspoons minced garlic
½ teaspoon dark sesame oil
½ teaspoon minced jalapeño pepper*

Jalapeño peppers can sting and irritate the skin; wear rubber gloves when handling peppers and do not touch eyes. Wash hands after handling.

Stir together CRISCO® Oil, sugar, sherry, garlic, sesame oil, pepper flakes and salt in a 13x9-inch baking dish. Stir until sugar is dissolved. Season steaks with salt and pepper. Add steaks, turning once to coat. Marinate for 1 hour, turning once.

To make Spicy Herb Sauce, stir together cilantro, CRISCO® Oil, soy sauce, lime juice, garlic, sesame oil and jalapeño; set aside.

Preheat grill.

Remove steaks from marinade. Discard marinade. Cook steaks on a medium-hot grill for 3 to 4 minutes per side for medium-rare or until desired doneness. Top each steak with sauce.   *Makes 6 servings*

Asian Grilled Steak with Spicy Herb Sauce

Eggplant Parmigiana

2 eggs, beaten
¼ cup milk
   Dash garlic powder
   Dash onion powder
   Dash salt
   Dash black pepper
1 large eggplant, cut into ½-inch-thick slices
½ cup seasoned dry bread crumbs
   Vegetable oil for frying
1 jar (about 26 ounces) pasta sauce
4 cups (16 ounces) shredded mozzarella cheese
2½ cups (10 ounces) shredded Swiss cheese
¼ cup grated Parmesan cheese
¼ cup grated Romano cheese

1. Preheat oven to 350°F. Combine eggs, milk, garlic powder, onion powder, salt and pepper in shallow bowl. Dip eggplant into egg mixture; coat in bread crumbs.

2. Add enough oil to large skillet to cover bottom by ¼ inch. Heat over medium-high heat. Brown eggplant in batches on both sides; drain on paper towels. Cover bottom of 13×9-inch baking dish with 2 or 3 tablespoons pasta sauce. Layer ½ of eggplant, ½ of mozzarella cheese, ½ of Swiss cheese and ½ of remaining sauce in dish. Repeat layers. Sprinkle with Parmesan and Romano cheeses.

3. Bake 30 minutes or until heated through and cheeses are melted.

Makes 4 servings

Eggplant Parmigiana

Champagne Scallops & Asparagus

10 large cloves garlic, peeled and halved
 2 tablespoons I CAN'T BELIEVE IT'S NOT BUTTER!® Spread
20 large sea scallops, rinsed and dried
 ¼ cup chopped shallots or onion
 ¼ cup apple juice or cider
 ¼ cup dry champagne or white wine
 1 tablespoon pure maple syrup or pancake syrup
 4 tablespoons finely chopped chives, divided
   Hot cooked rice
 1 pound asparagus, cooked
 1 tablespoon lemon juice

In small saucepan, cover garlic with water and bring to a boil over high heat. Boil 5 minutes. Drain garlic and set aside.

In 12-inch skillet, melt I Can't Believe It's Not Butter!® Spread over medium heat and cook 1 minute or until lightly golden. Add scallops and cook, stirring occasionally, 4 minutes or until scallops are opaque. Remove scallops and set aside.

In same skillet, stir in shallots, juice, champagne, maple syrup, garlic and 2 tablespoons chives. Bring to a boil over high heat. Continue boiling, scraping up any brown bits from bottom of skillet, until slightly thickened, about 2 minutes. On serving platter, arrange scallops over hot rice. Top with sauce and remaining chives. Serve with asparagus tossed with lemon juice. If desired, season with salt and ground black pepper.

Makes 4 servings

Champagne Scallops & Asparagus

Easy Beef Stroganoff

3 cans (10¾ ounces each) condensed cream of chicken or cream of
    mushroom soup, undiluted
1 cup sour cream
½ cup water
1 package (1 ounce) dry onion soup mix
2 pounds beef for stew

Slow Cooker Directions
Combine soup, sour cream, water and dry soup mix in slow cooker. Add
beef; stir until well coated. Cover; cook on on LOW 6 hours or HIGH
3 hours.   *Makes 4 to 6 servings*

Serving Suggestions: Serve the beef over hot cooked wild rice or noodles,
along with a salad and hot bread.

Chicken Pomodoro with Tomato Basil Garlic

4 teaspoons olive oil
8 boneless skinless chicken breast halves
8 ounces fresh mushrooms, sliced
2 cans (14¼ ounces each) Italian-style stewed tomatoes
8 teaspoons MRS. DASH® Tomato Basil Garlic Seasoning
½ cup semi-dry white wine (optional)

Heat oil in nonstick skillet. Add chicken and brown over medium heat
about 10 minutes, turning once. Add remaining ingredients. Bring to a
boil; reduce heat and simmer, uncovered, 15 minutes.   *Makes 8 servings*

Prep Time: 10 minutes
Cook Time: 25 minutes

Easy Beef Stroganoff

Vegetarian Lasagna

1 small eggplant, sliced into ½-inch rounds
½ teaspoon salt
2 tablespoons olive oil, divided
1 tablespoon butter
8 ounces mushrooms, sliced
1 small onion, diced
1 jar (26 ounces) pasta sauce
1 teaspoon dried basil leaves
1 teaspoon dried oregano leaves
2 cups part-skim ricotta cheese
1½ cups (6 ounces) shredded Monterey Jack cheese
1 cup grated Parmesan cheese, divided
1 package (8 ounces) whole wheat lasagna noodles, cooked and
    drained
1 medium zucchini, thinly sliced

Slow Cooker Directions

1. Sprinkle eggplant with salt; let sit 10 to 15 minutes. Rinse and pat dry; brush with 1 tablespoon olive oil. Brown on both sides in medium skillet over medium heat. Set aside.

2. Heat remaining 1 tablespoon olive oil and butter in same skillet over medium heat; cook and stir mushrooms and onion until softened. Stir in pasta sauce, basil and oregano. Set aside.

3. Combine ricotta cheese, Monterey Jack cheese and ½ cup Parmesan cheese in medium bowl. Set aside.

4. Spread ⅓ of sauce mixture in bottom of slow cooker. Layer with ⅓ of lasagna noodles, ½ of eggplant and ½ of cheese mixture. Repeat layers once. For last layer, use remaining ⅓ of lasagna noodles, zucchini, remaining ⅓ of sauce mixture and top with remaining ½ cup Parmesan.

5. Cover; cook on LOW 6 hours. Let sit 15 to 20 minutes before serving.
Makes 4 to 6 servings

Vegetarian Lasagna

Lemon Salmon and Spinach Pasta

¾ **pound salmon fillet**
 8 **ounces uncooked fettuccine**
 1 **teaspoon finely grated lemon peel**
¼ **teaspoon crushed red pepper**
 2 **cloves garlic, minced**
 4 **teaspoons butter**
 2 **tablespoons lemon juice**
 3 **cups washed baby spinach leaves**
½ **cup shredded carrot**

1. Rinse salmon; pat dry with paper towels. Remove skin from salmon; discard. Cut fish into ½-inch pieces.

2. Cook fettuccine according to package directions, omitting salt. Drain. Return to hot pan; set aside.

3. Meanwhile, melt butter in large skillet over medium-high heat. Add salmon, lemon peel, red pepper and garlic. Cook 4 to 7 minutes or until salmon flakes easily when tested with fork. Gently stir in lemon juice.

4. Add salmon mixture, spinach leaves and carrot to hot cooked linguine. Gently toss to combine. Serve immediately. *Makes 4 servings*

Prep Time: 15 minutes
Cook Time: 4 to 7 minutes

Helpful Hint

Fish fillets and steaks should have moist flesh that is free from discoloration and skin that is shiny and resilient. If the fillet or steak has a strong odor, it is not fresh.

Lemon Salmon and Spinach Pasta

Pesto-Coated Baked Chicken

1 pound boneless skinless chicken breasts, cut into ½-inch thick
    cutlets
¼ cup plus 1 tablespoon prepared pesto
1½ teaspoons sour cream
1½ teaspoons mayonnaise
  1 tablespoon grated Parmesan cheese
  1 tablespoon pine nuts

1. Preheat oven to 450°F. Arrange chicken in single layer in shallow
baking pan. Combine pesto, sour cream and mayonnaise in small cup.
Brush over chicken. Sprinkle with cheese and pine nuts.

2. Bake 8 to 10 minutes or until cooked through.   *Makes 4 servings*

Variation: Chicken can be cooked on an oiled grid over a preheated grill.

Grilled Garlic-Pepper Shrimp

⅓ cup olive oil
  2 tablespoons lemon juice
  1 teaspoon garlic pepper blend
20 jumbo shrimp, peeled and deveined
    Lemon wedges (optional)

1. Prepare grill for direct grilling.

2. Combine oil, lemon juice and garlic pepper in large resealable plastic
food storage bag; add shrimp. Marinate 20 to 30 minutes in refrigerator,
turning bag once.

3. Thread 5 shrimp onto each of 4 skewers; discard marinade. Grill on
grid over medium heat 6 minutes or until pink and opaque. Serve with
lemon wedges, if desired.   *Makes 4 servings*

Pesto-Coated Baked Chicken

Italian-Glazed Pork Chops

1 tablespoon olive oil
8 bone-in pork chops
1 medium zucchini, thinly sliced
1 medium red bell pepper, chopped
1 medium onion, thinly sliced
3 cloves garlic, finely chopped
¼ cup dry red wine or beef broth
1 jar (1 pound 10 ounces) RAGÚ® Chunky Gardenstyle Pasta Sauce

1. In 12-inch skillet, heat olive oil over medium-high heat and brown chops. Remove chops and set aside.

2. In same skillet, cook zucchini, red bell pepper, onion and garlic, stirring occasionally, 4 minutes. Stir in wine and Ragú Pasta Sauce.

3. Return chops to skillet, turning to coat with sauce. Simmer covered 15 minutes or until chops are tender and barely pink in the center. Serve, if desired, over hot cooked couscous or rice.   *Makes 8 servings*

Prep Time: 10 minutes
Cook Time: 25 minutes

Helpful Hint

When buying pork, look for meat that's pale pink with a small amount of marbling. The darker pink the flesh, the older the meat.

Italian-Glazed Pork Chop

Veggie Pie with Cucina Classica™ Parmesan Cheese

2 tablespoons olive oil
2 large carrots, thinly sliced
4 shallots,* sliced or 2 bunches (about 15) scallions, cut into
    ½-inch pieces
15 fresh green beans,* cut in half
6 eggs, beaten or 1½ cups egg substitute
½ cup low fat milk
1 tablespoon all-purpose flour
½ teaspoon salt
⅛ teaspoon pepper
½ cup CUCINA CLASSICA™ Grated Parmesan cheese

Medium yellow onion can be substituted for shallots and ½ cup peas can be substituted for green beans.

Preheat oven to 350°F. Grease 9-inch square baking dish or 9-inch quiche pan. Set aside.

In large skillet, heat olive oil over medium heat. Add carrots, shallots and beans. Cook 5 minutes or until shallots are glossy and carrots and beans are tender-crisp, stirring occasionally. Drain off any excess oil.

In large mixing bowl, mix eggs, milk, flour, salt, pepper and Cucina Classica™ Grated Parmesan cheese. Stir in vegetables. Pour into prepared baking dish. Bake 15 to 20 minutes or until set.   Makes 4 servings

Red Wine & Oregano Beef Kabobs

¼ cup finely chopped parsley
¼ cup dry red wine
2 tablespoons Worcestershire sauce
1 tablespoon reduced-sodium soy sauce
1 teaspoon dried oregano leaves
3 garlic cloves, minced
½ teaspoon salt (optional)
½ teaspoon black pepper
12 ounces boneless beef top sirloin steak, cut into 16 (1-inch) pieces
16 whole mushrooms (about 8 ounces total)
1 medium red onion, cut into eighths and layers separated

1. Combine parsley, wine, Worcestershire, soy sauce, oregano, garlic, salt, if desired, and pepper in small bowl; stir until well blended. Place steak, mushrooms and onion in resealable plastic food storage bag. Add wine mixture; toss. Seal bag; marinate in refrigerator 1 hour, turning frequently.

2. Soak 4 (12-inch) or 8 (6-inch) bamboo skewers in warm water for 20 minutes to prevent burning.

3. Preheat broiler. Alternate beef, mushrooms and 2 layers of onion on skewers.

4. Coat broiler rack with nonstick cooking spray. Arrange skewers on broiler rack; brush with marinade. Broil 4 to 6 inches from heat source 8 to 10 minutes, turning occasionally. *Makes 4 servings*

Chicken Vesuvio

1 whole chicken (about 3¾ pounds)
¼ cup olive oil
3 tablespoons lemon juice
4 cloves garlic, minced
3 large baking potatoes, peeled and cut lengthwise into quarters
Salt and lemon pepper

Preheat oven to 375°F. Place chicken, breast side down, on rack in large shallow roasting pan. Combine oil, lemon juice and garlic; brush half of oil mixture over chicken. Set aside remaining oil mixture. Roast chicken, uncovered, 30 minutes. Turn chicken, breast side up. Arrange potatoes around chicken in roasting pan. Brush chicken and potatoes with remaining oil mixture; season with salt and lemon pepper seasoning. Roast chicken and potatoes, basting occasionally with pan juices, 50 minutes or until meat thermometer inserted into thickest part of chicken thigh, not touching bone, registers 180°F.   *Makes 4 to 6 servings*

Steak with Mushroom Sauce

1½ pounds boneless beef sirloin steak
2 cups sliced fresh white mushrooms
1 medium onion, thinly sliced
1 (12-ounce) jar HEINZ® Fat Free Beef Gravy
1 tablespoon HEINZ® Tomato Ketchup
1 teaspoon HEINZ® Worcestershire Sauce
Dash pepper

Cut steak into 6 portions. Spray a large skillet with nonstick cooking spray. Cook steak over medium-high heat to desired doneness, about 5 minutes per side for medium rare. Remove and keep warm. In same skillet, cook mushrooms and onion until liquid evaporates. Stir in remaining ingredients; simmer 1 minute, stirring occasionally. Serve sauce over steak.

Makes 6 servings

Chicken Vesuvio

On the Side

Herbed Green Bean Casserole

   1 cup freshly grated Parmesan cheese
   ¾ cup dried bread crumbs
   2 teaspoons dried basil
   2 teaspoons dried parsley
   1 teaspoon dried oregano
   1 teaspoon garlic powder
   ½ teaspoon salt
   ½ teaspoon black pepper
   ½ teaspoon dried thyme
   ½ cup CRISCO® Oil
   2 (14-ounce) cans green beans, drained

Preheat oven to 350°F.

Combine first 9 ingredients in large bowl. Add CRISCO® Oil to bread crumb mixture; mix well. Reserve 2 tablespoons bread crumb mixture for top of casserole. Combine green beans and remaining bread crumb mixture in ovenproof dish; sprinkle with reserved crumb mixture.

Bake for about 30 minutes or until top is golden and crispy.

Makes 8 servings

Substitution: You can replace the canned beans with frozen or blanched and cooled fresh beans. The dried bread crumbs and herbs can be replaced with Italian-style bread crumbs.

Herbed Green Bean Casserole

Buttermilk Corn Bread Loaf

1½ cups all-purpose flour
1 cup yellow cornmeal
⅓ cup sugar
2 teaspoons baking powder
1 teaspoon salt
½ teaspoon baking soda
½ cup shortening
1⅓ cups buttermilk*
2 eggs

Or, substitute soured fresh milk. To sour milk, place 4 teaspoons lemon juice plus enough milk to equal 1⅓ cups in 2-cup measure. Stir; let stand 5 minutes before using.

1. Preheat oven to 375°F. Grease 8½×4½-inch loaf pan; set aside.

2. Combine flour, cornmeal, sugar, baking powder, salt and baking soda in medium bowl. Cut in shortening with pastry blender or 2 knives until mixture resembles coarse crumbs.

3. Whisk together buttermilk and eggs in small bowl. Make well in center of dry ingredients. Add buttermilk mixture; stir until mixture forms stiff batter. (Batter will be lumpy.) Turn into prepared pan; spread mixture evenly, removing any air bubbles.

4. Bake 50 to 55 minutes or until toothpick inserted in center comes out clean. Cool in pan on wire rack 10 minutes. Remove from pan; cool on rack 10 minutes more. Serve warm. *Makes 1 loaf (12 slices)*

Buttermilk Corn Bread Loaf

Sweet & Tangy Marinated Vegetables

8 cups mixed fresh vegetables, such as broccoli, cauliflower, zucchini, carrots and red bell peppers, cut into 1- to 1½-inch pieces
⅓ cup distilled white vinegar
¼ cup sugar
¼ cup water
1 packet (1 ounce) HIDDEN VALLEY® The Original Ranch® Salad Dressing & Seasoning Mix

Place vegetables in a gallon size Glad® Zipper Storage Bag. Whisk together vinegar, sugar, water and salad dressing & seasoning mix until sugar dissolves; pour over vegetables. Seal bag and shake to coat. Refrigerate 4 hours or overnight, turning bag occasionally.   *Makes 8 servings*

Cheese Bread

3 cups sifted all-purpose flour
1½ teaspoons ARM & HAMMER® Baking Soda
½ teaspoon salt
1½ cups low-sodium grated cheddar cheese
2 eggs
6 tablespoons white (distilled) vinegar, plus skim milk to make 1½ cups liquid
¼ cup melted shortening
1 teaspoon caraway seeds (optional)

Stir flour, Baking Soda and salt into mixing bowl. Add cheese; mix well. Beat eggs and combine with liquid and shortening; blend well. Stir in caraway seeds. Add all at once to flour mixture and mix lightly. Turn into greased 9×5-inch loaf pan. Bake at 350°F 70 minutes or until done. Remove from pan; cool several hours or overnight before slicing.

Makes 12 (¾-inch) slices

Sweet & Tangy Marinated Vegetables

Four Cheese Macaroni

1 package (16 ounces) uncooked macaroni
4 cups milk
4 cups (16 ounces) sharp white Cheddar cheese, shredded
4 cups (16 ounces) American cheese, shredded
2 cups (8 ounces) Muenster cheese, shredded
2 cups (8 ounces) mozzarella cheese, shredded
½ cup bread crumbs

1. Preheat oven to 350° F. Cook macaroni according to package directions. Drain; set aside and keep warm.

2. Heat milk in large saucepan over medium heat to almost boiling. Reduce heat to low. Gradually add cheeses, stirring constantly. Cook and stir about 5 minutes until all cheese has melted.

3. Place macaroni in 4-quart casserole or individual ovenproof dishes. Pour cheese sauce over pasta and stir until well blended. Sprinkle with bread crumbs. Bake 50 to 60 minutes or until browned and bubbly.

Makes 8 servings

Entertaining Idea

For a simple yet spectacular centerpiece any time of year, pick your favorite glass bowl and fill it with water. Place floating candles in the bowl with cranberries for winter, fresh cut flowers for summer and gourds for fall.

Four Cheese Macaroni

Savory Skillet Broccoli

1 tablespoon BERTOLLI® Olive Oil
6 cups fresh broccoli florets *or* 1 pound green beans, trimmed
1 envelope LIPTON® RECIPE SECRETS® Golden Onion Soup Mix*
1½ cups water

*Also terrific with LIPTON® RECIPE SECRETS® Onion-Mushroom Soup Mix.

1. In 12-inch skillet, heat oil over medium-high heat and cook broccoli, stirring occasionally, 2 minutes.

2. Stir in soup mix blended with water. Bring to a boil over high heat.

3. Reduce heat to medium-low and simmer covered 6 minutes or until broccoli is tender. *Makes 4 servings*

Prep Time: 5 minutes
Cook Time: 10 minutes

Asparagus with Goat Cheese Sauce

1 pound asparagus, trimmed

Goat Cheese Sauce
1 package (3½ ounces) goat cheese
2 cloves garlic, crushed
¾ cup chicken broth
¼ cup dry white wine
2 tablespoons chopped chives

1. Steam asparagus for 3 to 5 minutes or until crisp-tender.

2. While asparagus is steaming, prepare sauce. Mash cheese in a medium nonstick skillet and stir in garlic, broth and wine. Simmer over medium heat 8 to 10 minutes or until desired thickness, stirring frequently. Fold in chives; serve immediately over asparagus. *Makes 4 servings*

Savory Skillet Broccoli

Spiced Brown Bread Muffins

2 cups whole wheat flour
⅔ cup all-purpose flour
⅔ cup packed brown sugar
2 teaspoons baking soda
1 teaspoon pumpkin pie spice*
2 cups buttermilk
¾ cup raisins

Substitute ½ teaspoon ground cinnamon, ¼ teaspoon ground ginger and ⅛ teaspoon each ground allspice and ground nutmeg for 1 teaspoon pumpkin pie spice.

Preheat oven to 350°F. Grease 6 (4-inch) muffin cups. Combine flours, sugar, baking soda and pumpkin pie spice in large bowl. Stir in buttermilk just until flour mixture is moistened. Fold in raisins. Spoon into muffin cups. Bake 35 to 40 minutes until toothpick inserted into center comes out clean. Remove from pan.   *Makes 6 giant muffins*

Tomato Cheese Bread

1 can (14.5 ounces) CONTADINA® Recipe Ready Diced Tomatoes
2 cups buttermilk baking mix
2 teaspoons dried oregano leaves, crushed, divided
¾ cup (3 ounces) shredded Cheddar cheese
¾ cup (3 ounces) shredded Monterey Jack cheese

1. Drain tomatoes, reserving juice.

2. Combine baking mix, 1 teaspoon oregano and ⅔ cup reserved tomato juice in medium bowl.

3. Press dough evenly to edges of 11×7×2-inch greased baking dish. Sprinkle Cheddar cheese and remaining oregano over batter. Distribute tomato pieces evenly over cheese; sprinkle with Jack cheese.

4. Bake in preheated 375°F oven 25 minutes, or until edges are golden brown and cheese is bubbly. Cool 5 minutes before cutting into squares to serve.   *Makes 12 servings*

Spiced Brown Bread Muffin

Vegetables & Wild Rice

1 box UNCLE BEN'S® Long Grain & Wild Rice Roasted Garlic
2⅓ cups water
2 tablespoons butter or margarine
1 cup corn, fresh or frozen
1 medium tomato, chopped
4 strips bacon, cooked and crumbled
3 tablespoons chopped green onions

COOK: CLEAN: Wash hands. In medium skillet, combine water, butter, rice and contents of seasoning packet. Bring to a boil. Cover tightly and simmer 15 minutes. Add corn and simmer 15 minutes or until water is absorbed. Stir in tomato and bacon. Sprinkle with green onions.

SERVE: Serve with garlic toast, if desired.

CHILL: Refrigerate leftovers immediately.   *Makes 6 servings*

Garlic Onion Bread

½ cup butter or margarine, softened
2 tablespoons minced garlic
1 tablespoon chopped parsley
1 loaf (14 inches) Italian bread, split lengthwise in half
1⅓ cups *French's*® French Fried Onions
¼ cup grated Parmesan cheese

1. Preheat oven to 350°F. Mix butter, garlic and parsley. Spread half the butter mixture onto each cut side of bread. Sprinkle each with ⅔ *cup* French Fried Onions and 2 tablespoons cheese.

2. Place bread on baking sheet. Bake 5 minutes or until hot and onions are golden brown. Cut each half into 8 slices.   *Makes 8 servings*

Tip: You may substitute ⅔ cup prepared pesto sauce for the butter mixture.

Vegetables & Wild Rice

Crispy Onion Flat Breads

2½ cups all-purpose baking mix
  2 cups *French's*® French Fried Onions, divided
  1 cup shredded Cheddar cheese
  ¼ cup grated Parmesan cheese
  ½ cup water
  2 tablespoons *Frank's*® RedHot® Original Cayenne Pepper Sauce
  1 egg white, beaten

1. Combine baking mix, *⅔ cup* French Fried Onions and cheeses in large bowl. Stir in water and **Frank's RedHot** Sauce until mixture is blended (dough will be sticky). With hands, knead dough until it comes together and forms a ball. Press into 6-inch square and divide into 24 equal pieces; cover with plastic wrap.

2. Move 2 oven racks to lowest positions. Preheat oven to 325°F. Crush remaining onions. Roll each piece of dough to ¹⁄₁₆-inch thickness on well-floured surface. Place on parchment-lined or ungreased baking sheets. Brush dough with egg white; sprinkle with about 1 tablespoon crushed onions. Prick dough with fork several times.

3. Bake 15 to 17 minutes or until golden, rotating baking sheets from top to bottom. Cool flat breads on baking sheets for 1 minute. Transfer to cooling rack; cool completely. Flat breads may be stored in airtight container for up to 1 week.   *Makes 2 dozen flat breads*

Prep Time: 20 minutes
Cook Time: 17 minutes

Crispy Onion Flat Breads

Baked Risotto with Asparagus, Spinach & Parmesan

1 tablespoon olive oil
1 cup finely chopped onion
1 cup arborio (risotto) rice
8 cups (8 to 10 ounces) spinach leaves, torn into pieces
2 cups chicken broth
¼ teaspoon salt
¼ teaspoon ground nutmeg
½ cup grated Parmesan cheese, divided
1½ cups diagonally sliced asparagus

1. Preheat oven to 400°F. Spray 13×9-inch baking dish with nonstick cooking spray.

2. Heat olive oil in large skillet over medium-high heat. Add onion; cook and stir 4 minutes or until tender. Add rice; stir to coat with oil.

3. Stir in spinach, a handful at a time, adding more as it wilts. Add broth, salt and nutmeg. Reduce heat and simmer 7 minutes. Stir in ¼ cup cheese.

4. Transfer to prepared baking dish. Cover tightly and bake 15 minutes.

5. Remove from oven and stir in asparagus; sprinkle with remaining ¼ cup cheese. Cover and bake 15 minutes more or until liquid is absorbed.

Makes 6 servings

Baked Risotto with Asparagus, Spinach & Parmesan

Country Buttermilk Biscuits

2 cups all-purpose flour
1 tablespoon baking powder
2 teaspoons sugar
½ teaspoon baking soda
½ teaspoon salt
⅓ cup shortening
⅔ cup buttermilk*

*Or, substitute soured fresh milk. To sour milk, combine 2½ teaspoons lemon juice plus enough milk to equal ⅔ cup in a 1-cup measure. Stir; let stand 5 minutes before using.

1. Preheat oven to 450°F.

2. Combine flour, baking powder, sugar, baking soda and salt in medium bowl. Cut in shortening with pastry blender or 2 knives until mixture resembles coarse crumbs. Make well in center of dry ingredients. Add buttermilk; stir until mixture forms soft dough that clings together and forms ball.

3. Turn out dough onto well-floured surface. Knead dough gently 10 to 12 times. Roll or pat dough to ½-inch thickness. Cut out dough with floured 2½-inch biscuit cutter.

4. Place biscuits 2 inches apart on *ungreased* large baking sheet. Bake 8 to 10 minutes or until tops and bottoms are golden brown. Serve warm.

Makes about 9 biscuits

Drop Biscuits: Prepare Country Buttermilk Biscuits as directed in steps 1 and 2, except increase buttermilk to 1 cup. After adding buttermilk, stir batter with wooden spoon about 15 strokes. *Do not knead.* Drop dough by heaping tablespoonfuls, 1 inch apart, onto greased baking sheets. Bake as directed in step 4. Makes about 18 biscuits.

continued on page 98

Country Buttermilk Biscuits

Country Buttermilk Biscuits, *continued*

Sour Cream Dill Biscuits: Prepare Country Buttermilk Biscuits as directed in steps 1 and 2, except omit buttermilk. Combine ½ cup sour cream, ⅓ cup milk and 1 tablespoon chopped fresh dill or 1 teaspoon dried dill weed in small bowl until well blended. Stir into dry ingredients and continue as directed in steps 3 and 4. Makes about 9 biscuits.

Bacon 'n' Onion Biscuits: Prepare Country Buttermilk Biscuits as directed in steps 1 and 2, except add 4 slices crumbled crisply cooked bacon (about ⅓ cup) and ⅓ cup chopped green onions to flour-shortening mixture before adding buttermilk. Continue as directed in steps 3 and 4. Makes about 9 biscuits.

Ranch-Up!™ *Potato Wedges*

½ cup Wish-Bone® Ranch-Up!™ Classic, Zesty or Cheesy Dressing
4 medium all-purpose potatoes, cut into large wedges (about 2 pounds)
½ teaspoon ground black pepper

Preheat oven to 425°F. In 13×9-inch baking or roasting pan, combine all ingredients until evenly coated.

Bake uncovered, stirring occasionally, 40 minutes or until potatoes are tender and golden brown.

Serve with additional Ranch-Up!™ dressing for dipping.

Makes 4 servings

Prep Time: 10 minutes
Cook Time: 40 minutes

Tomato-Artichoke Focaccia

1 package (16 ounces) hot roll mix
2 tablespoons wheat bran
1¼ cups hot water
4 teaspoons olive oil, divided
1 cup thinly sliced onions
2 cloves garlic, minced
4 ounces dry sun-dried tomatoes, rehydrated* and cut into strips
1 cup canned artichoke hearts, sliced
1 tablespoon minced fresh rosemary
2 tablespoons freshly grated Parmesan cheese

To rehydrate sun-dried tomatoes, pour 1 cup boiling water over tomatoes in small heatproof bowl. Let tomatoes soak 5 to 10 minutes until softened; drain well.

1. Preheat oven to 400°F. Combine dry ingredients and yeast packet from hot roll mix in large bowl. Add bran; mix well. Stir in hot water and 2 teaspoons oil. Knead dough about 5 minutes or until ingredients are blended.

2. Spray 15½×11½-inch baking pan or 14-inch pizza pan with nonstick cooking spray. Press dough onto bottom of prepared pan. Cover; let rise 15 minutes.

3. Heat 1 teaspoon oil in medium skillet over low heat. Add onions and garlic; cook and stir 2 to 3 minutes until onions are tender.

4. Brush surface of dough with remaining 1 teaspoon oil. Top dough with onion mixture, tomatoes, artichokes and rosemary. Sprinkle with Parmesan.

5. Bake 25 to 30 minutes or until lightly browned on top. To serve, cut into 16 squares. Garnish each square with fresh rosemary sprigs, if desired.

Makes 16 servings

Spinach-Cheese Pasta Casserole

8 ounces uncooked pasta shells
2 eggs
1 cup ricotta cheese
1 package (10 ounces) frozen chopped spinach, thawed and
    squeezed dry
1 jar (26 ounces) marinara sauce
1 teaspoon salt
1 cup (4 ounces) shredded mozzarella cheese
¼ cup grated Parmesan cheese

1. Preheat oven to 350°F. Spray 1½-quart round casserole with nonstick cooking spray.

2. Cook pasta according to package directions until al dente. Drain.

3. Meanwhile, whisk eggs in large bowl until blended. Add ricotta and spinach to eggs; stir until combined. Stir in pasta, marinara sauce and salt until pasta is well coated. Pour into prepared dish. Sprinkle mozzarella and Parmesan evenly over casserole.

4. Bake, covered, 30 minutes. Uncover and bake 15 minutes or until hot and bubbly. *Makes 6 to 8 servings*

Helpful Hint

The next time you're making a casserole, assemble and bake two. Allow one to cool completely, then wrap it in heavy-duty foil and freeze it for another day. To reheat a frozen 2-quart casserole, unwrap it and microwave, covered, at HIGH for 20 to 30 minutes, stirring once or twice during cooking. Allow to stand about 5 minutes.

Spinach-Cheese Pasta Casserole

Italian Broccoli with Tomatoes

4 cups broccoli florets
½ cup water
2 medium tomatoes, cut into wedges
½ teaspoon dried Italian seasoning
½ teaspoon dried parsley flakes
¼ teaspoon salt (optional)
⅛ teaspoon black pepper
½ cup shredded part-skim mozzarella cheese

Microwave Directions

Place broccoli and water in 2-quart microwavable casserole; cover. Microwave at HIGH 5 to 8 minutes or until crisp-tender; drain. Stir in tomatoes, Italian seasoning, parsley, salt and pepper. Microwave, uncovered, at HIGH 2 to 4 minutes or until tomatoes are hot. Sprinkle with cheese. Microwave 1 minute or until cheese melts.   *Makes 6 servings*

Simple Savory Rice

2½ cups water
1 envelope LIPTON® RECIPE SECRETS® Soup Mix (any variety)
1 cup uncooked regular or converted rice

1. In 2-quart saucepan, bring water to a boil over high heat. Stir in soup mix and rice.

2. Reduce heat and simmer covered 20 minutes or until rice is tender.
                                                Makes 3 servings

Prep Time: 5 minutes
Cook Time: 25 minutes

Italian Broccoli with Tomatoes

Basil Biscuits

2 cups all-purpose flour
4 tablespoons grated Parmesan cheese, divided
1 tablespoon baking powder
½ teaspoon baking soda
¼ teaspoon salt (optional)
4 tablespoons Neufchâtel cheese
2 tablespoons butter, divided
6 ounces plain nonfat yogurt
⅓ cup slivered fresh basil leaves

1. Combine flour, 2 tablespoons Parmesan, baking powder, baking soda and salt in large bowl. Cut in Neufchâtel and 1 tablespoon butter with pastry blender or two knives until mixture forms coarse crumbs. Stir in yogurt and basil, mixing just until dough clings together. Turn dough out onto lightly floured surface and gently pat into ball. Knead just until dough holds together. Pat and roll dough into 7-inch log. Cut into 7 (1-inch-thick) slices.

2. Spray 10-inch cast iron skillet or Dutch oven with nonstick cooking spray; arrange biscuits in skillet. Melt remaining 1 tablespoon butter and brush over biscuit tops. Sprinkle with remaining 2 tablespoons Parmesan. Place skillet on grid set 4 to 6 inches above medium-hot coals (about 375°F); cover grill. Bake 20 to 40 minutes or until golden and firm on top.

Makes 7 biscuits

Note: To prepare a charcoal grill for baking, arrange a single, solid, even layer of medium coals in bottom of charcoal grill. If necessary, reduce temperature by either allowing coals to cook down or removing 3 or 4 coals at a time to a fireproof container until desired temperature is reached. For a gas grill, begin on medium heat and adjust heat as necessary. Besides raising or lowering the temperature setting, you can turn off one side of the grill or set each side to a different temperature.

Basil Biscuits

Ravishing Desserts

Chocolate Malt Delights

1 package (18 ounces) refrigerated chocolate chip cookie dough
⅓ cup plus 3 tablespoons malted milk powder, original or chocolate
    flavor, divided
1¼ cups prepared chocolate frosting
1 cup coarsely chopped malted milk balls

1. Preheat oven to 350°F. Grease cookie sheets.

2. Remove dough from wrapper; place in large bowl. Let dough stand at room temperature about 15 minutes.

3. Add ⅓ cup malted milk powder to dough in bowl; beat at medium speed of electric mixer until well blended. Drop rounded tablespoonfuls of dough onto cookie sheet.

4. Bake 10 to 12 minutes or until lightly browned at edges. Cool on cookie sheets 5 minutes; remove to wire racks to cool completely.

5. Combine frosting and remaining 3 tablespoons malted milk powder. Top each cookie with rounded tablespoonful of frosting; garnish with malted milk balls. *Makes about 1½ dozen cookies*

Chocolate Malt Delights

Easy Raspberry Ice Cream

8 ounces (1¾ cups) frozen unsweetened raspberries
2 to 3 tablespoons powdered sugar
½ cup whipping cream

1. Place raspberries in food processor fitted with steel blade. Process using on/off pulsing action about 15 seconds or until raspberries resemble coarse crumbs.

2. Add sugar; process using on/off pulsing action until smooth. With processor running, add cream, processing until well blended. Serve immediately.   *Makes 3 servings*

Variation: Substitute other berries for the raspberries.

Bananas Foster

6 tablespoons I CAN'T BELIEVE IT'S NOT BUTTER!® Spread
3 tablespoons firmly packed brown sugar
4 medium ripe bananas, sliced diagonally
2 tablespoons dark rum or brandy (optional)
  Vanilla ice cream

In 12-inch skillet, bring I Can't Believe It's Not Butter!® Spread, brown sugar and bananas to a boil. Cook 2 minutes, stirring gently. Carefully add rum to center of pan and cook 15 seconds. Serve hot banana mixture over scoops of ice cream and top, if desired, with sweetened whipped cream.
                                        Makes 4 servings

Note: Recipe can be halved.

Prep Time: 5 minutes
Cook Time: 5 minutes

Easy Raspberry Ice Cream

Chocolate Ice Cream Cups

1 (12-ounce) package semi-sweet chocolate chips (2 cups)
1 (14-ounce) can EAGLE BRAND® Sweetened Condensed Milk
   (NOT evaporated milk)
1 cup finely ground pecans
   Ice cream, any flavor

1. In heavy saucepan over low heat, melt chips with EAGLE BRAND®; remove from heat. Stir in pecans. In individual paper-lined muffin cups, spread about 2 tablespoons chocolate mixture. With lightly greased spoon, spread chocolate on bottom and up side of each cup.

2. Freeze 2 hours or until firm. Before serving, remove paper liners. Fill chocolate cups with ice cream. Store unfilled cups tightly covered in freezer. *Makes about 1½ dozen cups*

Note: It is easier to remove the paper liners if the chocolate cups sit at room temperature for about 5 minutes first.

BelGioioso® Mascarpone Chocolate Pie

16 ounces BELGIOIOSO® Mascarpone
2½ tablespoons ground chocolate or grated chocolate chips
2 small bananas plus more for garnish, sliced
1 graham cracker pie shell
24 semi-sweet chocolate chips or ½ cup grated chocolate

In a small mixing bowl, mix BelGioioso Mascarpone with ground chocolate. Place 2 sliced bananas on bottom of pie shell and top with Mascarpone mixture. Garnish with remaining banana slices and chocolate chips or grated chocolate. *Makes 8 servings*

Chocolate Ice Cream Cups

Apple Crunch Pie

1 refrigerated pie crust (½ of 15-ounce package)
1¼ cups all-purpose flour, divided
1 cup granulated sugar
6 tablespoons butter, melted and divided
1½ teaspoons ground cinnamon, divided
¾ teaspoon ground nutmeg, divided
½ teaspoon ground ginger
¼ teaspoon salt
4 cups peeled, cored, diced apples
½ cup packed brown sugar
½ cup chopped walnuts

1. Preheat oven to 350°F. Place crust in 9-inch pie pan; flute edge as desired.

2. Combine ¼ cup flour, granulated sugar, 2 tablespoons butter, 1 teaspoon cinnamon, ½ teaspoon nutmeg, ginger and salt; mix well. Add apples; toss to coat. Place apple mixture in crust.

3. Combine remaining 1 cup flour, 4 tablespoons butter, ½ teaspoon cinnamon, ¼ teaspoon nutmeg, brown sugar and walnuts in small bowl. Sprinkle evenly over apple mixture.

4. Bake 45 to 55 minutes or apples are tender.   *Makes 8 servings*

Helpful Hint

*To prevent major oven cleanups, place juicy
fruit pies on a baking sheet while baking.*

Apple Crunch Pie

Reese's® Double Peanut Butter and Milk Chocolate Chip Cookies

½ cup (1 stick) butter or margarine, softened
¾ cup sugar
⅓ cup REESE'S® Creamy or Crunchy Peanut Butter
1 egg
½ teaspoon vanilla extract
1¼ cups all-purpose flour
½ teaspoon baking soda
¼ teaspoon salt
1¾ cups (11-ounce package) REESE'S® Peanut Butter and Milk
   Chocolate Chips

1. Heat oven to 350°F.

2. Beat butter, sugar and peanut butter in medium bowl until creamy. Add egg and vanilla; beat well. Stir together flour, baking soda and salt; add to butter mixture, blending well. Stir in chips. Drop by rounded teaspoons onto ungreased cookie sheets.

3. Bake 12 to 14 minutes or until light golden brown around the edges. Cool 1 minute on cookie sheets. Remove to wire rack; cool completely.

Makes about 3 dozen cookies

Reese's® Double Peanut Butter and Milk Chocolate Chip Cookies

Cinnamon Swirls

1 package (18 ounces) refrigerated sugar cookie dough
½ cup packed light brown sugar
2 teaspoons ground cinnamon
1 cup powdered sugar
2 to 3 tablespoons milk
½ cup finely chopped walnuts or pecans (optional)

1. Remove dough from wrapper; divide dough in half. Wrap 1 dough half in plastic wrap; refrigerate. Place remaining dough half in medium bowl; let stand at room temperature about 15 minutes.

2. Add brown sugar and cinnamon to dough in bowl; beat at medium speed of electric mixer until well blended. Wrap dough in plastic wrap; refrigerate until needed.

3. Roll plain dough on lightly floured surface to form 8-inch square. Repeat with cinnamon dough; place cinnamon dough on top of plain dough. Roll up doughs into 10-inch log. Wrap log in plastic wrap; freeze at least 1 hour before slicing.

4. Preheat oven to 350°F. Grease cookie sheets. Cut dough log into ⅜-inch slices; place on prepared cookie sheets. Bake 10 to 12 minutes or until cookies are lightly browned. Remove to wire racks; cool completely.

5. For icing, mix powdered sugar and 2 tablespoons milk in small bowl until smooth; add additional milk to reach drizzling consistency if necessary. Drizzle icing over cooled cookies; sprinkle with nuts, if desired.

Makes 2 dozen cookies

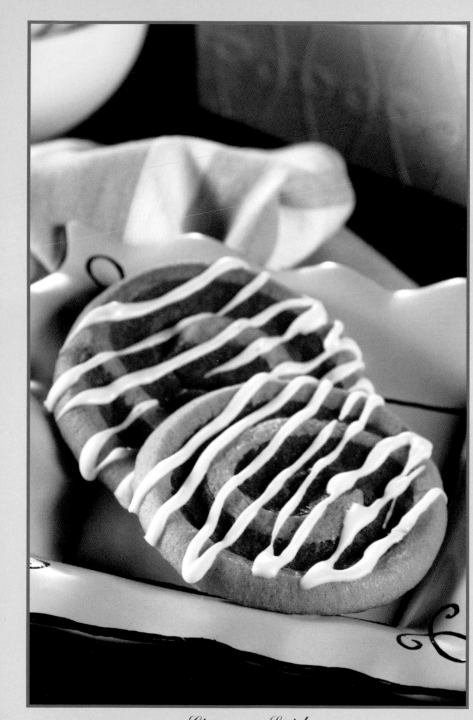

Cinnamon Swirls

Brownie Bites

1 package (18 ounces) refrigerated chocolate chip cookie dough
with fudge filling in squares or rounds (20 count)
¼ cup unsweetened cocoa powder
1½ teaspoons vanilla, divided
1 package (18 ounces) refrigerated chocolate chip cookie dough
4 ounces cream cheese (½ cup), softened
1 cup sifted powdered sugar

1. Grease 30 mini (1¾-inch) muffin pan cups. Remove chocolate chip and fudge cookie dough from wrapper; place in large bowl. Let dough stand at room temperature about 15 minutes.

2. Add cocoa and ½ teaspoon vanilla to dough in bowl; beat at medium speed of electric mixer until well blended. Shape dough into 30 balls; press onto bottoms and up sides of prepared muffin cups. Refrigerate 1 hour.

3. Preheat oven to 350°F. Remove chocolate chip cookie dough from wrapper. Shape into 30 balls. Place each chocolate chip ball into dough-lined muffin cups. Gently flatten tops if necessary. Bake 14 to 16 minutes. Cool in pans 10 minutes. Remove to wire racks; cool completely.

4. Combine cream cheese and remaining 1 teaspoon vanilla in medium bowl. Beat at medium speed of electric mixer, gradually adding powdered sugar until frosting is light and fluffy. Spoon heaping teaspoonful frosting onto each cookie.   *Makes 2½ dozen cookies*

Helpful Hint

*Brownie Bites are best served the day they
are made; leftovers should be refrigerated.*

Brownie Bites

Chocolate Chip-Oat Cookies

1 package (about 18 ounces) yellow cake mix
1 teaspoon baking powder
¾ cup vegetable oil
2 eggs
1 teaspoon vanilla
1 cup uncooked old-fashioned oats
¾ cup semisweet chocolate chips

1. Preheat oven to 350°F. Lightly grease cookie sheets or line with parchment paper.

2. Stir together cake mix and baking powder in large bowl. Add oil, eggs and vanilla; beat by hand until well blended. Stir in oats and chocolate chips.

3. Drop dough by slightly rounded tablespoonfuls, 2 inches apart, onto prepared cookie sheets. Bake 10 minutes or until golden brown. *Do not overbake.*

4. Cool on cookie sheets 5 minutes; remove to wire rack to cool completely. *Makes 4 dozen cookies*

Entertaining Idea

Savor your dessert later. Why rush into a spectacular dessert right after a fabulous meal when everyone is still stuffed from dinner. Retire to the living room where dessert and coffee can be served. Everyone can relax and enjoy each other's company.

Chocolate Chip-Oat Cookies

Pineapple Daiquiri Sundae

1 pineapple, cored, peeled, and cut into ½-inch chunks
½ cup sugar
½ cup dark rum
3 tablespoons lime juice
 Peel of 2 limes, cut in long strands
1 tablespoon cornstarch or arrowroot

Slow Cooker Directions
Place all ingredients in slow cooker; mix well. Cover; cook on HIGH 3 to 4 hours. Serve hot over ice cream, pound cake or shortcakes. Garnish with a few fresh raspberries and mint leaves, if desired.   *Makes 4 to 6 servings*

Variation: Substitute 1 can (20 ounces) crushed pineapple, drained, for the fresh pineapple. Cook on HIGH 3 hours.

Granny Smith Crisp

5 cups peeled, cored and sliced Granny Smith apples
½ cup sugar
1 teaspoon ground cinnamon
 Streusel Topping (recipe follows)

Heat oven to 350°F. In large bowl, toss apples with sugar and cinnamon; spread apple mixture in 11×8-inch baking pan. Prepare Streusel Topping; spread evenly over apples. Bake 35 to 40 minutes or until apples are tender.   *Makes 6 servings*

Streusel Topping: In medium bowl, combine ¾ cup all-purpose flour, ¼ cup granulated sugar and ¼ cup packed brown sugar. With pastry blender or 2 knives, cut in ½ cup (1 stick) butter until crumbly mixture is formed. Stir in ½ cup quick rolled oats.

Favorite recipe from **Washington Apple Commission**

Pineapple Daiquiri Sundae

Mini Chocolate Cheesecakes

3 packages (8 ounces each) cream cheese, softened
½ cup sugar
3 eggs
1 teaspoon vanilla
8 squares (1 ounce each) semisweet baking chocolate

1. Preheat oven to 325°F. Lightly grease 12 (2¾-inch) muffin pan cups; set aside.

2. Beat cream cheese and sugar about 2 minutes in large bowl with electric mixer at medium speed until light and fluffy. Add eggs and vanilla; beat about 2 minutes until well blended.

3. Place chocolate in 1-cup microwavable bowl. Microwave at HIGH 1 to 1½ minutes or until chocolate is melted, stirring after 1 minute. Beat melted chocolate into cream cheese mixture until well blended.

4. Divide mixture evenly among prepared muffin cups. Place muffin pan in larger baking pan; place on oven rack. Pour warm water into larger pan to depth of ½ to 1 inch. Bake cheesecakes 30 minutes or until edges are dry and centers are almost set. Remove muffin pan from water. Cool cheesecakes completely in muffin pan on wire rack.   *Makes 12 servings*

Mini Swirl Cheesecakes: Before adding chocolate to batter in mixer bowl, place about 2 heaping tablespoons of batter into each muffin cup. Add chocolate to remaining batter in mixer bowl and beat to combine. Spoon chocolate batter on top of vanilla batter in muffin cups. Swirl with a knife before baking.

Mini Swirl Cheesecakes

Rich Caramel Cake

1 (14-ounce) package caramels, unwrapped
½ cup (1 stick) butter or margarine
1 (14-ounce) can EAGLE BRAND® Sweetened Condensed Milk
    (NOT evaporated milk)
1 (18.25- or 18.5-ounce) package chocolate cake mix, plus
    ingredients to prepare mix
1 cup coarsely chopped pecans

1. Preheat oven to 350°F. In heavy saucepan over low heat, melt caramels and butter. Remove from heat; add EAGLE BRAND®. Mix well. Set aside caramel mixture. Prepare cake mix as package directs.

2. Spread 2 cups cake batter into greased 13×9-inch baking pan; bake 15 minutes. Spread caramel mixture evenly over cake; spread remaining cake batter over caramel mixture. Top with pecans. Return to oven; bake 30 to 35 minutes or until cake springs back when lightly touched. Cool.

Makes 10 to 12 servings

Chocolate Peanut Butter Pie

1 can (14 ounces) sweetened condensed milk
¼ cup creamy peanut butter
2 tablespoons unsweetened cocoa powder
1 container (8 ounces) nondairy frozen whipped topping, thawed
1 (6-ounce) chocolate cookie crumb crust

1. Beat condensed milk, peanut butter and cocoa in large bowl with electric mixer until smooth and well blended. Fold in whipped topping. Pour mixture into crust.

2. Freeze at least 6 hours or overnight. Garnish as desired.

Makes 7 to 8 servings

Rich Caramel Cake

Chocolate Magic Mousse Pie

1 envelope unflavored gelatin
2 tablespoons water
¼ cup boiling water
1 cup sugar
½ cup HERSHEY'S Cocoa
2 cups (1 pint) cold whipping cream
2 teaspoons vanilla extract
1 packaged graham cracker crumb crust (6 ounces)
   Refrigerated whipped light cream in pressurized can
   HERSHEY'S MINI KISSES® Milk Chocolates

1. Sprinkle gelatin over cold water in small bowl; let stand 2 minutes to soften. Add boiling water; stir until gelatin is completely dissolved and mixture is clear. Cool slightly.

2. Mix sugar and cocoa in large bowl; add whipping cream and vanilla. Beat on medium speed, scraping bottom of bowl often, until mixture is stiff. Pour in gelatin mixture; beat until well blended. Spoon into crust. Refrigerate about 3 hours. Garnish with whipped cream and chocolate pieces. Store, covered, in refrigerator. *Makes 6 to 8 servings*

Prep Time: 5 minutes

Helpful Hint

Run a finger over the spoon to test for undissolved granules. If it is smooth, the gelatin is completely dissolved; if it feels granular, place in microwave and heat until it feels smooth.

Chocolate Magic Mousse Pie

Angel Cake with Almond Butter Sauce

 1 prepared angel food cake (14 ounces)
 8 ounces sliced almonds
 2 cups (4 sticks) butter
14 packages sugar substitute
 1 teaspoon ground cinnamon
 ½ teaspoon ground nutmeg

1. Preheat oven to 325°F.

2. Cut cake into 16 slices with serrated knife. Arrange cake slices accordion-fashion on ovenproof serving plate. Cover with foil; bake 10 minutes or until heated through.

3. Meanwhile, place 12-inch nonstick skillet over medium-high heat until hot. Add almonds; cook and stir 4 minutes or until lightly browned. Remove from pan; set aside.

4. Heat butter in same skillet over medium heat until bubbly. Remove from heat; stir in sugar substitute, cinnamon and nutmeg.

5. Sprinkle cake evenly with almonds. Spoon butter mixture over cake.

Makes 16 servings

Angel Cake with Almond Butter Sauce

Marshmallow Brownie Bars

1 package (about 21 ounces) brownie mix plus ingredients to
    prepare mix
2½ cups miniature marshmallows
½ cup (1 stick) butter
4 tablespoons unsweetened cocoa powder
⅓ cup cola
1 teaspoon vanilla
4 cups powdered sugar
1 cup chopped nuts (almonds, peanuts, pecans or walnuts)

1. Prepare brownies according to package directions for 13×9-inch pan. Remove from oven and immediately top with single layer of marshmallows. Place under broiler until marshmallows begin to brown.

2. Combine butter, cocoa powder and cola in medium saucepan. Cook and stir over medium heat until mixture comes to a boil. Remove from heat; add vanilla and stir until smooth. Add powdered sugar and nuts and stir 1 to 2 minutes more or until well combined. Pour over marshmallows and spread to coat evenly. *Makes about 18 brownies*

Helpful Hint

Make these brownies in a disposable aluminum pan. When you are ready to serve, cut down the sides of the pan and peel away. Cut the brownies into squares and discard the pan.

Mocha No-Bake Cookies

1 package (9 ounces) chocolate wafer cookies
1/3 cup light corn syrup
1/3 cup coffee-flavored liqueur
1 cup finely chopped walnuts, toasted
3/4 cup powdered sugar
3 tablespoons unsweetened cocoa powder
Chocolate-covered coffee beans (optional)

1. Break half of cookies in half; place in food processor. Process using on/off pulses until fine crumbs form. Transfer to small bowl and set aside. Repeat with remaining cookies. Combine corn syrup and liqueur in medium bowl; mix well. Stir in crumbs and walnuts; mix well.

2. Combine powdered sugar and cocoa in small bowl; mix well. Combine 1/2 cup of cocoa mixture with cookie crumb mixture; mix well. Reserve remaining cocoa mixture for coating.

3. Roll dough into 1-inch balls with oiled hands. Cover and chill at least 3 hours or up to 3 days before serving. Roll each ball in remaining cocoa mixture to coat; transfer to plate. Garnish each cookie with chocolate-covered coffee bean, if desired. Serve chilled or at room temperature.

Makes about 3 dozen cookies

Rich Chocolate Mousse

1 cup (6 ounces) NESTLÉ® TOLL HOUSE® Semi-Sweet Chocolate
   Morsels
3 tablespoons butter, cut into pieces
2 teaspoons TASTER'S CHOICE® 100% Pure Instant Coffee
1 tablespoon hot water
2 teaspoons vanilla extract
½ cup heavy whipping cream

MICROWAVE morsels and butter in medium, uncovered, microwave-safe bowl on HIGH (100%) power for 1 minute. STIR. Morsels may retain some of their original shape. If necessary, microwave at additional 10- to 15-second intervals, stirring just until morsels are melted. Dissolve Taster's Choice in hot water; stir into chocolate. Stir in vanilla extract; cool to room temperature.

WHIP cream in small mixer bowl on high speed until stiff peaks form; fold into chocolate mixture. Spoon into tall glasses; refrigerate for 1 hour or until set. Garnish as desired. *Makes 2 servings*

Rich Chocolate Mousse

No-Bake Fudgy Brownies

1 (14-ounce) can EAGLE BRAND® Sweetened Condensed Milk
(NOT evaporated milk)
2 (1-ounce) squares unsweetened chocolate, cut up
1 teaspoon vanilla extract
2 cups plus 2 tablespoons packaged chocolate cookie crumbs,
divided
¼ cup miniature candy-coated milk chocolate pieces or chopped
nuts

1. Grease 8-inch square baking pan or line with foil; set aside.

2. In medium heavy saucepan over low heat, combine EAGLE BRAND®
and chocolate; cook and stir just until boiling. Reduce heat; cook and stir
for 2 to 3 minutes more or until mixture thickens. Remove from heat. Stir
in vanilla.

3. Stir in 2 cups cookie crumbs. Spread evenly in prepared pan. Sprinkle
with remaining cookie crumbs and chocolate pieces or nuts; press down
gently with back of spoon.

4. Cover and chill 4 hours or until firm. Cut into squares. Store covered
in refrigerator.   *Makes 24 to 36 bars*

Prep Time: 10 minutes
Chill Time: 4 hours

No-Bake Fudgy Brownies

Strawberry Raspberry Cake

1 package DUNCAN HINES® Moist Deluxe® Strawberry Supreme
Cake Mix
2 ounces white chocolate baking bar, grated, divided
½ cup red raspberry jam
1 container DUNCAN HINES® Creamy Home-Style Classic Vanilla
Frosting
Red raspberries (optional)

1. Preheat oven to 350°F. Grease and flour two 9-inch round cake pans.

2. Prepare cake mix as directed on package. Stir in ½ cup grated chocolate. Set aside remaining chocolate for garnish. Bake at 350°F for 28 to 31 minutes or until toothpick inserted in center comes out clean. Cool in pans 15 minutes. Invert onto cooling racks. Cool completely.

3. Place one cake layer on serving plate. Spread with jam. Top with second cake layer. Frost sides and top of cake with frosting. Garnish with remaining grated chocolate and raspberries.   *Makes 12 to 16 servings*

Entertaining Idea

*Tight on space? If you are afraid your table
is too small to accommodate all your quests,
avoid using place mats. Use a table cloth or
nothing at all. This will help you to be able
to put place settings closer together.*

Chocolate Caramel Brownies

1 package (18.25 ounces) chocolate cake mix
1 cup chopped nuts
½ cup (1 stick) butter or margarine, melted
1 cup NESTLÉ® CARNATION® Evaporated Milk, *divided*
35 caramels (10-ounce package), unwrapped
2 cups (12-ounce package) NESTLÉ® TOLL HOUSE® Semi-Sweet Chocolate Morsels

PREHEAT oven to 350°F.

COMBINE cake mix and nuts in large bowl. Stir in butter and ⅔ *cup* evaporated milk (batter will be thick). Spread *half* of batter into greased 13×9-inch baking pan.

BAKE for 15 minutes.

HEAT caramels and *remaining* evaporated milk in small saucepan over low heat, stirring constantly, until caramels are melted. Sprinkle morsels over brownies; drizzle with caramel mixture.

DROP *remaining* batter by heaping teaspoon over caramel mixture.

BAKE for 25 to 30 minutes or until center is set. Cool in pan on wire rack.

Makes 24 brownies

Bottoms Up Beverages

Mulled Cranberry Tea

2 tea bags
1 cup boiling water
1 bottle (48 ounces) cranberry juice
½ cup dried cranberries (optional)
⅓ cup sugar
1 large lemon, cut into ¼-inch slices
4 cinnamon sticks
6 whole cloves
    Additional thin lemon slices for garnish
    Additional cinnamon sticks for garnish

Slow Cooker Directions

1. Place tea bags in slow cooker. Pour boiling water over tea bags; cover and let stand 5 minutes. Remove and discard tea bags. Stir in cranberry juice, cranberries, if desired, sugar, lemon slices, 4 cinnamon sticks and cloves. Cover; cook on LOW 2 to 3 hours or on HIGH 1 to 2 hours.

2. Remove and discard lemon slices, cinnamon sticks and cloves. Serve in warm mugs with additional fresh lemon slice and cinnamon stick.

Makes 8 servings

Prep Time: 10 minutes
Cook Time: 2 to 3 hours (LOW) • 1 to 2 hours (HIGH)

Mulled Cranberry Tea

Piña Colada Punch

　　3 cups water
　10 whole cloves
　　4 cardamom pods
　　2 sticks cinnamon
　　1 can (12 ounces) frozen pineapple juice concentrate, thawed
　　1 pint low-fat piña colada frozen yogurt, softened*
1¼ cups lemon seltzer water
1¼ teaspoons rum extract
　¾ teaspoon coconut extract (optional)

Or, substitute pineapple sherbet for low-fat piña colada frozen yogurt. When using pineapple sherbet, use coconut extract for more authentic flavor.

1. Combine water, cloves, cardamom and cinnamon in small saucepan. Bring to a boil over high heat; reduce heat to low. Simmer, covered, 5 minutes; cool. Strain and discard spices.

2. Combine spiced water, pineapple juice concentrate and frozen yogurt in small punch bowl or pitcher. Stir until frozen yogurt is melted. Stir in seltzer water, rum extract and coconut extract, if desired. Garnish with mint sprigs, if desired.　　　　　*Makes 12 (4-ounce) servings*

Daiquiri

　¾ cup MAUNA LA'I® ¡Mango Mango!® Juice Drink
　3 tablespoons rum
　1 tablespoon ROSE'S® Lime Juice
　1 teaspoon sugar
　　Ice, as needed

Combine Mauna La'i ¡Mango Mango! Juice Drink, rum, lime juice and sugar in shaker with ice. Pour into tall glass filled with ice.

Makes 1 drink

Piña Colada Punch

Chai Tea

2 quarts (8 cups) water
8 bags black tea
¾ cup sugar*
16 whole cloves
16 whole cardamom seeds, pods removed (optional)
5 cinnamon sticks
8 slices fresh ginger
1 cup milk

Chai Tea is typically a sweet drink. For less sweet tea, reduce sugar to ½ cup.

Slow Cooker Directions

1. Combine water, tea, sugar, cloves, cardamom, cinnamon and ginger in slow cooker. Cover; cook on HIGH 2 to 2½ hours.

2. Strain mixture; discard solids. (At this point, tea may be covered and refrigerated up to 3 days).

3. Stir in milk just before serving. Serve warm or chilled.

Makes 8 to 10 servings

Prep Time: 8 minutes
Cook Time: 2 to 2½ hours

Entertaining Idea

When serving warm beverages at your party, an easy way to keep them warm without the fuss of standing over the stove is to put them in a slow cooker turned on low. Simply place mugs and ladle near the slow cooker so guests can help themselves.

Chai Tea

Nectarine Mocktail

3 fresh California nectarines, halved, pitted and diced
1 container (10 ounces) unsweetened frozen strawberries, partially
    thawed
1 bottle (28 ounces) club soda or sugar-free ginger ale
8 mint sprigs (optional)

Add nectarines, strawberries and 1 cup club soda to blender. Process until smooth. Pour into chilled glasses about ⅔ full. Top with remaining club soda. Garnish with mint, if desired. *Makes 8 servings*

Favorite recipe from **California Tree Fruit Agreement**

Mojito

6 packets NatraTaste® Brand Sugar Substitute
2 cups very hot water
4 to 6 mint leaves
¼ cup fresh lime juice
2 ounces light or dark rum
½ cup seltzer or club soda
   Ice cubes

1. Combine the NatraTaste® and water in a jar or container with a lid; shake.

2. Place the mint leaves in the bottom of two glasses and press down with a spoon to release the flavor. Divide lime juice and rum between glasses. Add ¼ cup *each* sweetened water and seltzer to each glass. Add ice cubes and stir. *Makes 2 servings*

Note: Refrigerate remaining sweetened water for future use.

Nectarine Mocktail

Strawberry Champagne Punch

2 packages (10 ounces each) frozen sliced strawberries in syrup, thawed
2 cans (5½ ounces each) apricot or peach nectar
¼ cup lemon juice
2 tablespoons honey
2 bottles (750 ml each) champagne or sparkling white wine, chilled

1. Place strawberries with syrup in food processor; process until smooth.

2. Pour puréed strawberries into large punch bowl. Stir in apricot nectar, lemon juice and honey; blend well. Refrigerate until serving time.

3. To serve, stir champagne into strawberry mixture.   *Makes 12 servings*

Cutting Corners: To save time, thaw the strawberries in the refrigerator the day before using them.

Prep Time: 15 minutes

Honey Lemonade

Concentrate
   6 tablespoons honey
   1 cup lemon juice
   1 lemon, thinly sliced

Mixer
   Ice cubes
   1 quart carbonated water

For concentrate, dissolve honey in lemon juice in 1-quart jar or glass bowl. Add lemon slices and refrigerate until ready to use.

For mixer, fill 12-ounce glass with ice cubes. Add ¼ cup lemon juice concentrate and fill glass with carbonated water.   *Makes 4 servings*

Tip: Garnish with a lemon wedge.

Favorite recipe from **National Honey Board**

Strawberry Champagne Punch

Kiwi Margarita

3½ ounces MR & MRS T® Margarita Mix
2 ripe kiwi, peeled
1 cup strawberry sorbet
1½ ounces white rum
2 ounces club soda
1 lime, sliced
MR & MRS T® Margarita Salt (optional)

Blend first 5 ingredients in blender on low speed until smooth.* Coat rim of glass with lime and dip in margarita salt, if desired. Pour into glass.

Makes 1 serving

Be careful not to blend too long, as crushed kiwi seeds taste bitter.

Tangy Sangria

1 bottle (750 ml) red wine
2 ounces brandy
2 ounces Triple Sec
2 teaspoons sugar
2 teaspoons fresh lime juice
2 teaspoons fresh orange juice
½ teaspoon TABASCO® brand Pepper Sauce
½ orange, thinly sliced
½ lemon, thinly sliced
1 (16-ounce) bottle sparkling water

Combine red wine, brandy, Triple Sec, sugar, lime juice, orange juice, TABASCO® Sauce and fruit slices in pitcher. Chill.

To serve, fill large wine glasses with ice. Pour ⅔ full with sangría and top with sparkling water.

Makes 6 to 8 servings

Mango Margarita (page 153),
Kiwi Margarita and Daiquiri (page 142)

Icy Mimosas

6 cloth napkins, optional
6 wine goblets, preferably frozen
3 cups frozen Tropic Ice, crushed (recipe follows)
3 cups diet ginger ale or Champagne
6 frozen whole strawberries with stems attached

Tie napkin around stem of each wine goblet, if desired. Prepare Tropic Ice. Spoon ½ cup crushed Tropic Ice in each goblet. Pour ½ cup ginger ale over each serving and add 1 frozen strawberry.   *Makes 6 servings*

Tropic Ice

4 cups tropical fruit juice, such as pineapple, orange and banana
1 (12-ounce) can diet ginger ale
¾ cup frozen white grape juice concentrate
½ cup dry white wine, such as Chardonnay (see note)

1. Place all ingredients in gallon resealable freezer plastic bag. Place in freezer overnight or until frozen.

2. To serve, place bag on counter. Pound with meat mallet to break up large pieces of frozen mixture or use fork to scrape frozen mixture into slush. Store remaining frozen mixture in freezer until needed. Mixture can be made ahead of time and stored in freezer up to 1 month.

Makes 10 cups

Note: The alcohol in the wine keeps the mixture from freezing solid. If you choose not to use the wine, the mixture will be harder, but can still be scraped with a fork or broken up with a mallet, after thawing slightly. You can also chop the ice in a food processor to make a slush.

Triple Delicious Hot Chocolate

⅓ cup sugar
¼ cup unsweetened cocoa powder
¼ teaspoon salt
3 cups milk, divided
¾ teaspoon vanilla
1 cup heavy cream
1 square (1 ounce) bittersweet chocolate
1 square (1 ounce) white chocolate
¾ cup whipped cream
6 teaspoons mini chocolate chips or shaved bittersweet chocolate

Slow Cooker Directions

1. Combine sugar, cocoa, salt and ½ cup milk in medium bowl. Beat until smooth. Pour into slow cooker. Add remaining 2½ cups milk and vanilla. Cover; cook on LOW 2 hours.

2. Add cream. Cover and cook on LOW 10 minutes. Stir in bittersweet and white chocolate until melted.

3. Pour hot chocolate into 6 mugs. Top each with 2 tablespoons whipped cream and 1 teaspoon chocolate chips. *Makes 6 servings*

Mango Margarita

½ cup MAUNA LA'I® ¡Mango Mango!® Juice Drink
1 ounce tequila
  Dash ROSE'S® Triple Sec
  Dash ROSE'S® Lime Juice
  Ice, as needed
  Lime wedge

Combine Mauna La'i ¡Mango Mango! Juice Drink, tequila, triple sec and lime juice in shaker with ice. Pour into salt-rimmed margarita glass. Garnish with lime. *Makes 1 drink*

Acknowledgments

The publisher would like to thank the companies and organizations listed below for the use of their recipes and photographs in this publication.

Arm & Hammer Division, Church & Dwight Co., Inc.

Alouette® Cheese, Chavrie® Cheese, Saladena®

BelGioioso® Cheese, Inc.

California Tree Fruit Agreement

Crisco is a registered trademark of The J.M. Smucker Company

Cucina Classica Italiana, Inc.

Del Monte Corporation

Duncan Hines® and Moist Deluxe® are registered trademarks of Pinnacle Foods Corp.

Eagle Brand® Sweetened Condensed Milk

The Golden Grain Company®

Heinz North America

Hershey Foods Corporation

The Hidden Valley® Food Products Company

Jif® trademark of The J.M. Smucker Company

Keebler® Company

Lawry's® Foods

MASTERFOODS USA

Mauna La'i® is a registered trademark of Mott's, LLP

McIlhenny Company (TABASCO® brand Pepper Sauce)

Mr & Mrs T® is a registered trademark of Mott's, LLP

Mrs. Dash®

National Honey Board

NatraTaste® is a registered trademark of Stadt Corporation

Nestlé USA

Perdue Farms Incorporated

Reckitt Benckiser Inc.

Sargento® Foods Inc.

Unilever Foods North America

US Highbush Blueberry Council

Walnut Marketing Board

Washington Apple Commission

A

Alouette Garlic and Herb Croustade, 42

Angel Cake with Almond Butter Sauce, 130

Angel Wings, 42

Apple Crunch Pie, 112

Apples

Apple Crunch Pie, 112

Granny Smith Crisp, 122

Spiced Pancakes with Apple Topping, 10

Apricot

Apricot BBQ Glazed Shrimp and Bacon, 38

Apricot Ginger Dipping Sauce, 46

Bodacious Grilled Ribs, 52

Strawberry Champagne Punch, 148

Walnut-Crusted Salmon Bites with Apricot Ginger Dipping Sauce, 46

Apricot BBQ Glazed Shrimp and Bacon, 38

Apricot Ginger Dipping Sauce, 46

Asian Grilled Steaks with Spicy Herb Sauce, 58

Asparagus

Asparagus with Goat Cheese Sauce, 86

Baked Risotto with Asparagus, Spinach & Parmesan, 94

Champagne Scallops & Asparagus, 62

Asparagus with Goat Cheese Sauce, 86

B

Bacon

Alouette Garlic and Herb Croustade, 42

Apricot BBQ Glazed Shrimp and Bacon, 38

Bacon 'n' Onion Biscuits, 98

Bacon (*continued*)

Individual Spinach & Bacon Quiches, 24

Vegetables & Wild Rice, 90

Bacon 'n' Onion Biscuits, 98

Baked Risotto with Asparagus, Spinach & Parmesan, 94

Bananas

Bananas Foster, 108

BelGioioso® Mascarpone Chocolate Pie, 110

Bananas Foster, 108

Basil Biscuits, 104

Beef

Asian Grilled Steaks with Spicy Herb Sauce, 58

Easy Beef Stroganoff, 64

Red Wine & Oregano Beef Kabobs, 75

Steak with Mushroom Sauce, 76

BelGioioso® Mascarpone Chocolate Pie, 110

Bodacious Grilled Ribs, 52

Broccoli

Italian Broccoli with Tomatoes, 102

Savory Skillet Broccoli, 86

Brownie Bites, 118

Brownies

Brownie Bites, 118

Chocolate Caramel Brownies, 139

Marshmallow Brownie Bars, 132

No-Bake Fudgy Brownies, 136

Brunch Sausage Casserole, 22

Buffalo Chicken Wing Sampler, 30

Buttermilk Corn Bread Loaf, 80

C

Cakes

Angel Cake with Almond Butter Sauce, 130

Donut Spice Cakes, 4

Cakes (*continued*)
Mini Chocolate Cheesecakes, 124
Mini Swirl Cheesecakes, 124
Rich Caramel Cake, 126
Strawberry Raspberry Cake, 138
California Veggie Rolls, 28
Carrots
California Veggie Rolls, 28
Lemon Salmon and Spinach Pasta, 68
Veggie Pie with Cucina Classica™ Parmesan Cheese, 74
Chai Tea, 144
Champagne Scallops & Asparagus, 62
Cheese Bread, 82
Chicken
Angel Wings, 42
Buffalo Chicken Wing Sampler, 30
Chicken Pomodoro with Tomato Basil Garlic, 64
Chicken Vesuvio, 76
Marinated Chicken Satay with Peanut Butter Dipping Sauce, 37
Pesto-Coated Baked Chicken, 70
RedHot® Sampler Variations, 30
Saucy Tomato Chicken, 54
Chicken Pomodoro with Tomato Basil Garlic, 64
Chicken Vesuvio, 76
Chile Rellenos Monte Cristos, 14
Chocolate (*see also* **Chocolate, Baking; Chocolate Chips**)
Brownie Bites, 118
Chocolate Caramel Brownies, 139
Chocolate Ice Cream Cups, 110
Chocolate Magic Mousse Pie, 128
Chocolate Malt Delights, 106
Chocolate Peanut Butter Pie, 126
Marshmallow Brownie Bars, 132
Mocha No-Bake Cookies, 133
Rich Caramel Cake, 126

Chocolate Caramel Brownies, 139
Chocolate Chip-Oat Cookies, 120
Chocolate Chips
BelGioioso® Mascarpone Chocolate Pie, 110
Chocolate Caramel Brownies, 139
Chocolate Chip-Oat Cookies, 120
Donna's Heavenly Orange Chip Scones, 12
Lots o' Chocolate Bread, 20
Reese's® Double Peanut Butter and Milk Chocolate Chip Cookies, 114
Rich Chocolate Mousse, 134
Triple Delicious Hot Chocolate, 153
Chocolate Ice Cream Cups, 110
Chocolate Magic Mousse Pie, 128
Chocolate Malt Delights, 106
Chocolate Peanut Butter Pie, 126
Chocolate, Baking
Mini Chocolate Cheesecakes, 124
Mini Swirl Cheesecakes, 124
No-Bake Fudgy Brownies, 136
Cinnamon Spiced Muffins, 16
Cinnamon Swirls, 116
Cookies
Chocolate Chip-Oat Cookies, 120
Chocolate Malt Delights, 106
Cinnamon Swirls, 116
Mocha No-Bake Cookies, 133
Reese's® Double Peanut Butter and Milk Chocolate Chip Cookies, 114
Country Buttermilk Biscuits, 96
Crab Cakes with Horseradish Mustard Sauce, 34
Cranberry
Mini Pumpkin Cranberry Breads, 6
Mulled Cranberry Tea, 140
Crispy Onion Flat Breads, 92

D
Daiquiri, 142
Donna's Heavenly Orange Chip
    Scones, 12
Donut Spice Cakes, 4
Drop Biscuits, 96

E
Easy Beef Stroganoff, 64
Easy Raspberry Ice Cream, 108
Eggplant Parmigiana, 60

F
Fish
    Grilled Tequila Lime Salmon, 48
    Lemon Salmon and Spinach Pasta,
        68
    Walnut-Crusted Salmon Bites with
        Apricot Ginger Dipping Sauce, 46
Four Cheese Macaroni, 84

G
Garlic Onion Bread, 90
Granny Smith Crisp, 122
Green Beans
    Herbed Green Bean Casserole, 78
    Veggie Pie with Cucina Classica™
        Parmesan Cheese, 74
Grilled Garlic-Pepper Shrimp, 70
Grilled Tequila Lime Salmon, 48

H
Ham
    Ham and Swiss Quiche, 8
    Mini-Quiche Appetizers, 8
Ham and Swiss Quiche, 8
Hash Brown Bake, 22
Hawaiian Fruit and Nut Quick Bread,
    26
Herbed Green Bean Casserole, 78
Honey Lemonade, 148

Huevos Rancheros in Tortilla Cups,
    23

I
Icy Mimosas, 152
Individual Spinach & Bacon Quiches,
    24
Italian Broccoli with Tomatoes, 102
Italian-Glazed Pork Chops, 72

K
Kiwi Margarita, 150

L
Lemon Salmon and Spinach Pasta, 68
Lots o' Chocolate Bread, 20

M
Mango Margarita, 153
Marinated Chicken Satay with Peanut
    Butter Dipping Sauce, 37
Marshmallow Brownie Bars, 132
Mediterranean Roast Tomatoes, 44
Mediterranean Sausage and Spinach
    Tartlets, 47
Mini Chocolate Cheesecakes, 124
Mini Pumpkin Cranberry Breads, 6
Mini-Quiche Appetizers, 8
Mini Swirl Cheesecakes, 124
Mocha No-Bake Cookies, 133
Mojito, 146
Mulled Cranberry Tea, 140
Mushrooms
    Alouette Garlic and Herb Croustade,
        42
    Chicken Pomodoro with Tomato
        Basil Garlic, 64
    Red Wine & Oregano Beef Kabobs,
        75
    Steak with Mushroom Sauce, 76
    Vegetarian Lasagna, 66

N

Nectarine Mocktail, 146

No-Bake Fudgy Brownies, 136

Noodles & Pasta

 Four Cheese Macaroni, 84

 Lemon Salmon and Spinach Pasta, 68

 Saucy Tomato Chicken, 54

 Seafood Parmesan, 56

 Spinach-Cheese Pasta Casserole, 100

 Vegetarian Lasagna, 66

Nuts

 Angel Cake with Almond Butter Sauce, 130

 Apple Crunch Pie, 112

 Chocolate Caramel Brownies, 139

 Hawaiian Fruit and Nut Quick Bread, 26

 Marshmallow Brownie Bars, 132

 Mocha No-Bake Cookies, 133

 Rich Caramel Cake, 126

 Walnut-Crusted Salmon Bites with Apricot Ginger Dipping Sauce, 46

O

Orange: Donna's Heavenly Orange Chip Scones, 12

P

Parmesan Turkey Breast, 50

Peanut Butter

 Chocolate Peanut Butter Pie, 126

 Marinated Chicken Satay with Peanut Butter Dipping Sauce, 37

 Reese's® Double Peanut Butter and Milk Chocolate Chip Cookies, 114

Pesto-Coated Baked Chicken, 70

Pies

 Apple Crunch Pie, 112

 Chocolate Magic Mousse Pie, 128

Piña Colada Punch, 142

Pineapple Daiquiri Sundae, 122

Pork (*see also* **Bacon; Ham; Sausage**)

 Bodacious Grilled Ribs, 52

 Italian-Glazed Pork Chops, 72

Potatoes

 Chicken Vesuvio, 76

 Ranch-Up!™ Potato Wedges, 98

Pumpkin: Mini Pumpkin Cranberry Breads, 6

R

Ranch-Up!™ Potato Wedges, 98

Raspberry

 Easy Raspberry Ice Cream, 108

 Strawberry Raspberry Cake, 138

Red Wine & Oregano Beef Kabobs, 75

RedHot® Sampler Variations, 30

Reese's® Double Peanut Butter and Milk Chocolate Chip Cookies, 114

Rice

 Baked Risotto with Asparagus, Spinach & Parmesan, 94

 Simple Savory Rice, 102

 Vegetables & Wild Rice, 90

Rich Caramel Cake, 126

Rich Chocolate Mousse, 134

S

Santa Fe Shrimp Martini Cocktails, 36

Saucy Tomato Chicken, 54

Sausage

 Brunch Sausage Casserole, 22

 Mediterranean Sausage and Spinach Tartlets, 47

Savory Skillet Broccoli, 86

Scallops: Champagne Scallops &
  Asparagus, 62
Seafood Parmesan, 56
Shrimp
  Apricot BBQ Glazed Shrimp and
    Bacon, 38
  Grilled Garlic-Pepper Shrimp, 70
  Santa Fe Shrimp Martini Cocktails,
    36
  Seafood Parmesan, 56
Simple Savory Rice, 102
Sour Cream Dill Biscuits, 98
Spiced Brown Bread Muffins, 88
Spiced Pancakes with Apple Topping,
  10
Spinach
  Baked Risotto with Asparagus,
    Spinach & Parmesan, 94
  California Veggie Rolls, 28
  Individual Spinach & Bacon
    Quiches, 24
  Lemon Salmon and Spinach Pasta,
    68
  Mediterranean Sausage and Spinach
    Tartlets, 47
  Spinach-Artichoke Party Cups, 40
  Spinach-Cheese Pasta Casserole,
    100
Spinach-Artichoke Party Cups, 40
Spinach-Cheese Pasta Casserole, 100
Steak with Mushroom Sauce, 76
Strawberry
  Icy Mimosas, 152
  Kiwi Margarita, 150
  Nectarine Mocktail, 146
  Strawberry Champagne Punch, 148
  Strawberry Raspberry Cake, 138
Strawberry Champagne Punch, 148
Strawberry Raspberry Cake, 138
Stuffed French Toast with Fresh Berry
  Topping, 18

Sweet & Tangy Marinated Vegetables,
  82

T
Tangy Sangria, 150
Tomato and Caper Crostini, 32
Tomato-Artichoke Focaccia, 99
Tomato Cheese Bread, 88
Triple Delicious Hot Chocolate, 153
Tropic Ice, 152
Turkey: Parmesan Turkey Breast, 50

V
Vegetables & Wild Rice, 90
Vegetarian Lasagna, 66
Veggie Pie with Cucina Classica™
  Parmesan Cheese, 74

W
Walnut-Crusted Salmon Bites with
  Apricot Ginger Dipping Sauce, 46

METRIC CONVERSION CHART

VOLUME MEASUREMENTS (dry)

1/8 teaspoon = 0.5 mL
1/4 teaspoon = 1 mL
1/2 teaspoon = 2 mL
3/4 teaspoon = 4 mL
1 teaspoon = 5 mL
1 tablespoon = 15 mL
2 tablespoons = 30 mL
1/4 cup = 60 mL
1/3 cup = 75 mL
1/2 cup = 125 mL
2/3 cup = 150 mL
3/4 cup = 175 mL
1 cup = 250 mL
2 cups = 1 pint = 500 mL
3 cups = 750 mL
4 cups = 1 quart = 1 L

VOLUME MEASUREMENTS (fluid)

1 fluid ounce (2 tablespoons) = 30 mL
4 fluid ounces (1/2 cup) = 125 mL
8 fluid ounces (1 cup) = 250 mL
12 fluid ounces (1 1/2 cups) = 375 mL
16 fluid ounces (2 cups) = 500 mL

WEIGHTS (mass)

1/2 ounce = 15 g
1 ounce = 30 g
3 ounces = 90 g
4 ounces = 120 g
8 ounces = 225 g
10 ounces = 285 g
12 ounces = 360 g
16 ounces = 1 pound = 450 g

DIMENSIONS

1/16 inch = 2 mm
1/8 inch = 3 mm
1/4 inch = 6 mm
1/2 inch = 1.5 cm
3/4 inch = 2 cm
1 inch = 2.5 cm

OVEN TEMPERATURES

250°F = 120°C
275°F = 140°C
300°F = 150°C
325°F = 160°C
350°F = 180°C
375°F = 190°C
400°F = 200°C
425°F = 220°C
450°F = 230°C

BAKING PAN SIZES

Utensil	Size in Inches/Quarts	Metric Volume	Size in Centimeters
Baking or	8×8×2	2 L	20×20×5
Cake Pan	9×9×2	2.5 L	23×23×5
(square or	12×8×2	3 L	30×20×5
rectangular)	13×9×2	3.5 L	33×23×5
Loaf Pan	8×4×3	1.5 L	20×10×7
	9×5×3	2 L	23×13×7
Round Layer	8×1½	1.2 L	20×4
Cake Pan	9×1½	1.5 L	23×4
Pie Plate	8×1¼	750 mL	20×3
	9×1¼	1 L	23×3
Baking Dish	1 quart	1 L	—
or Casserole	1½ quart	1.5 L	—
	2 quart	2 L	—